The Facts About Work Addiction

GOOD NEWS FOR THE WORK ADDICT

"There are no complex psychiatric analyses . . . there are no elaborate social hypotheses. . . . Instead, the book is refreshingly personalized, based on one person's astute observations of daily and downtown existence. Unencumbered by professionalism, the book offers a unique insight into human nature."—**Cross and Crown**

"Here is sound advice for those who go at top speed day in and day out, with all too often fatal results. It is a must book."—**The Christian**

"Top executive, minister, housewife—whatever your station in life, you must pause long enough from your work to read this book."—**Provident Book Review**

"This book will make you smile, but if the shoe fits, it will also make you wince! If you are a workaholic, you can be cured. Read the book and see how!"—**Moody Monthly**

Confessions of a Workaholic

The Facts About Work Addiction

Wayne E. Oates

ABINGDON

Nashville

99-096

Scripture quotations are from the Revised Standard
Version Common Bible, copyrighted © 1973.

CONFESSIONS OF A WORKAHOLIC

A Festival Book

Copyright © 1971 by Wayne Oates

ISBN 0-687-09393-7

Printed in the United States of America

To

Clarence Y. Barton, Th.M.
John H. Boyle, Th.D.
D. Swan Haworth, Ph.D.
Elizabeth Hutchens, Ed.D.

Preface

I have written the following pages as a serious jest. Laughter, ridicule, cynicism, sarcasm, irony, caricature, and poignancy appear here and there. I hope the reader recognizes this and does not take me so seriously that he cannot chuckle with me. On the other hand, I hope that he can take me seriously enough to know that often laughter, especially laughter at oneself, is earned at the price of pain. I have paid some of that bill, I think, which gives me the right to laugh at myself as a person compelled to work, and to attempt to josh my reader out of the habit, too. But I hope for heaven's sake that my reader seasons what I have said with a grain of salty humor.

I am indebted to Guy Brown for originally encouraging me to write this book. His investment of confidence is an inspiration to me. I also appreciate the careful editorial advice and detailed assistance given to me by Richard Marek of World Publishing. My family—my wife, my sons, and our daughter-in-law—have provided an atmosphere of conversation and rollicking happiness as I have written these pages. My colleagues, to whom the book is dedicated, have given me both serious and humorous insight into myself as a worker while I have sought to formulate these ideas.

Wayne E. Oates

Contents

Contents

I
The Workaholic:
It Takes One to Catch One

Workaholism is a word which I have invented. It is not in your dictionary. It means addiction to work, the compulsion or the uncontrollable need to work incessantly. Workaholism has hidden beginnings in economic, cultural, and emotional deprivation in childhood. It becomes acute in the presence of institutional deprivation of approval and appreciation in the second and third decades of life. It also becomes aggravated in health crises and interpersonal crises of the forties and early fifties. If it is not reversed or arrested in the forties and early fifties, it becomes chronic and may lead to death in one form or another in the late fifties and/or sixties.

You ask me: "How do you know?" I answer: "I know because I was a workaholic myself."

I am not going to kid you or play games with you about it. Insofar as the printed word permits, I want to meet my readers face to face. The pages of this book are a thinly disguised autobiography of a "converted" workaholic. The conversion does not change the basic personality formation of the workaholic; it only releases the power of the addiction. Once released from slavery to work, a person is enabled to recognize it in others more clearly. He never does so with pride because he knows that the moment he becomes complacent about his own uprightness, he is about to fall into his old habits again. Therefore, this chapter begins the book with a confession of a workaholic, a "working" definition of workaholism, and a description of the syndrome or collection of symptoms that identify a dyed-in-the-wool workaholic.

A Confession of a Workaholic

Most of us try to help alcoholics when we have the opportunity to do so, but we have a hard time understanding and identifying with them. When I meet an alcoholic, I am likely to respond to him as if he were a breed apart, completely different from me. Yet I learned from people who spend all their time working with alcoholics that I should face up to the fact that in some ways I was similarly addicted. I began to examine my own patterns of behavior carefully. I had to admit to myself and to those with whom I work that I have an addiction, too. Although it is far more socially acceptable than alcohol or drug addiction, it is nevertheless an addiction. It is more profitable than drug addiction, let us say (unless you are a pusher as well as a user), or than alcoholism (unless you wholesale the stuff as well as drink it). Nevertheless, when it comes to being a human being, workaholism is an addiction that can be almost equally destructive.

When the truth first dawned upon me that I am a work addict, two important things happened immediately. First, I broke into laughter. The realization was too true to be anything but painfully funny. I refuse to give up this grace of laughing at myself, because it keeps the truth from knocking me down long enough for me to begin to do something about my situation. I would encourage my reader to laugh along with me and beg of him not to laugh *at* me. Because the louder he laughs the more likely he is to be a workaholic himself, rejoicing in the evil he has found in me that relieves him of the painful necessity of taking heed of his own plight. Second, I discovered a whole community of suffering among other people who either heard me talk of my addiction or read a brief article I wrote in the October, 1968, issue of *Pastoral Psychology.*

Most significant in the community of suffering that I discovered were the alcoholics and drug addicts whom I came to understand and appreciate more. I discovered I have a ground of common human frailty to stand upon *with* the alcoholic and the drug addict. I, like them, must admit that I am powerless to "kick the habit" and must ask God's help. I must "hit bottom" in desperation about the overinvolvement I have in my place of work. I had to come to terms with the problem of overcommitment. This overcommitment for me was a sort of idolatry of the job I had. It even passed itself off as a kind of religious devotion. Actually it was a false religion, an addiction to work for its own sake. Wrapped up in my own habituation to work was my self-sufficiency as a "doer" who trusts fully in my own work. Ensconced in my always-at-it work pattern was the hidden assumption that I was indispensable. The outfit for which I worked, I felt, could not really get along without me. I kept reinforcing this feeling with around-the-clock activity, as if the whole operation depended on me. This was not so. It was an illusion. I eventually admitted it.

When I did, I confessed to my limitations, finiteness, and humanity. Yet childish feelings of omnipotence fought with the confession. I as a workaholic, like an alcoholic, found that admitting my humanness called for an acceptance of my own powerlessness and helplessness. This created a feeling of need for help from others and from God. This need, in turn, was met by many people around me, most especially members of my family. The good news is that a real community was waiting, available, and responsive.

I have been astonished to see how many people begin immediately to respond with their own confessions when I spell out what I mean by workaholism. Other kinds of addicts—alcoholics, drug addicts, etc.—are amazed when I admit to them my habituation to work. As I have said, I find other people who have painted themselves into impossible corners on their jobs and they become a part of the community of the addicted I have described. All of us together can sustain each other by reinforcing each other's commitment to "kick the habit" of defying the day's doing as a means of survival. For me, probably the most rewarding discovery of fresh community with persons has been among members of my own family. For years they have tried to lure me away from work to enjoy a time of effortless play with them. Now they are convinced that what they have been trying to tell me for years is finally being heard. In fact, life is more livable now both for them and me.

A Definition of Workaholism

Naturally, the word "workaholism" is a neologism, an invented word, a semihumorous word for addiction to work. Howard Clinebell says "that dependence on *overwork* (work compulsion) and dependence upon overeating (food addiction) are psychologically very similar to drug dependency."[1] When we look at classical definitions of the term "addiction" we begin to get a more serious understanding of *workaholism*. Addiction means the condition of applying habitually, of giving oneself up or over to as a constant practice, of devoting oneself or habituating oneself to something. This general dictionary definition can mean anything and everything, but a narrower use of the term is made by the World Health Organization with specific reference to alcohol addiction. Such addicts "are those excessive drinkers whose dependence upon alcohol has attained such a degree that it shows a noticeable mental disturbance or interference with their bodily and mental health, interpersonal relations, and their smooth social and economic functioning."[2] A definition of the workaholic along similar lines would say that he is a person

[1] *The Pastor and Drug Dependency* (New York: Council Press, 1968), p. 9.
[2] Expert Committee on Mental Health, Alcoholism Subcommittee, 2nd Report, World Health Organization Technical Report Series, No. 48, August 1952.

whose need for work has become so excessive that it creates noticeable disturbance or interference with his bodily health, personal happiness, and interpersonal relations, and with his smooth social functioning.

Yet there is a fundamental distinction to be made between workaholism and alcohol and drug addiction, which involves the degree to which the addiction varies from the norms of the community and culture. Our culture has a very different attitude toward the alcoholic from the one it has toward overwork. Excessive work is lauded, praised, expected, and often demanded of a person in America. In fact, one of the main criteria for determining whether a person is mentally disturbed is whether or not he or she is able to function effectively on the job. This says little or nothing about the workaholic who often is so very effective at work that he becomes isolated and at odds with his community, albeit much less obviously and more insidiously than when he "drops out of the human community" through the use of alcohol or some of the more exotic drugs. Workaholism is a much more socially approved malady than alcoholism, though both have crippling manifestations, and is more difficult to deal with.

Work, furthermore, can become the special addiction of the religious man. The monks of Cluny could say that "to work is to pray." This meant something quite different, however, from saying that work itself is the god to whom we pray, the god whom we propitiate with our bodies for the sins of our spirits, the idol who enslaves us. Addiction to work is not far from the disorder of the monasteries known as *acedia,* earlier classified by Johannes Cassianus (*ca.* 5th century A.D.) as one of the seven deadly sins. *Acedia* was defined by Evagius Ponticus as the condition in a monk that made him fall asleep in his cell or else desert his religious work altogether. It stemmed from the fact that the religious man's work had gone beyond the point of increasing returns: he worked more and more and accomplished less and less, becoming all the while more and more bored with and anxious over his work.

Mark D. Altschule says that in contemporary life *acedia* has dropped out of common usage and the psychiatric concept of depressions has taken its place. Erik Erikson identifies this kind of depression as a "work paralysis" in which a person has striven so hard and achieved so long that the organism rebels and refuses to produce any more.[3] As I have said, this dark distemper of the spirit easily develops in the religious man's situation, especially in a works-oriented expression of the religious life such as is prevalent in American Christianity. For us indeed the very religion we espouse puts such a value on work that we feel more religious the more we are addicted to work! The religious group tends to extol this form of addiction. The community in general sees the work addict only from afar, in terms of what he or she gets done, expressing "oohs" and "ahs" of amazement at the workaholic's accomplishments.

A Description of Workaholism

The best way to describe workaholism or work addiction is to discuss the developmental phases of the malady. The history of a workaholic at first is no different from that of other working people. Many people regard work as a necessary evil, a part of the human condition, and some people tend to look upon it as the special penalty laid upon us because of the disobedience of Adam and Eve in the Garden of Eden. We take very seriously the words of God

---

[3] Mark D. Altschule, "Acedia: Its Evolution from Deadly Sin to Psychiatric Syndrome," *British Journal of Psychiatry,* III (1965), 117-19.

to Adam and Eve: "In the sweat of your face you shall eat bread till you return to the ground" (Genesis 3:19*a*). Even though we give work a "holy glow," a religious halo, in our hearts we tend to look upon it as a sort of punishment; our sense of guilt is transformed into anxiety-laden work that can propitiate what we unconsciously perceive to be an angry God. In relation to our fellow men, we also quite consciously use work as a means of securing their pity— we "work ourselves to death," or "into an early grave"— and of gaining their approval; and as a means of outdoing them in competition. In these several senses, work can be vaguely described as a characteristic of the whole human race.

Thus, the first expression of workaholism is indistinguishable from honest industry in all men. We all work, as millions of men drink today: on a *social* basis. There is nothing inherently wrong with work. Everybody sooner or later gets around to it even if only in the form of exertion to avoid work! For years the average worker goes along enjoying his work, sharing his work with others, talking shop on evening social occasions, and swapping work stories with his fellow workers. There is such a thing as work being play, and many people can take their work or leave it, without *having* to have it in order to be happy or to survive as a person, or without being driven to it like a quarry slave in the bondage of a compulsion to work. However, in such crowds of people there are premonitory signs of the developing workaholic.

The Early or Prodromal Phase of Workaholism

The stream of speech of an emerging workaholic will tend to betray the true trend toward workaholism. First, at a party he (or she) will inevitably tell others how *early* he came to work or how *late* he remained. As in other disorders, this means that the next thing you hear will be how *little sleep* he has been getting. The difference here is that instead of getting worried about such an individual the community usually begins to compare him with Thomas Edison or some other genius. This person may begin by spending the hours of a regular working day drinking coffee (to counteract having lost sleep the night before), in bull sessions, et cetera. Then he is forced to use the hours other people use for parties and for sleeping to catch up on work left undone during the day. If this person happens to be a housewife, she may spend several hours during the ordinary workday in long telephone conversations. Then she has to burn the midnight oil getting the day's work done. However, this is not the picture given in conversation. Instead, the person *boasts* about how early he arose or how late he stayed up or how little sleep he got.

The second symptom of early workaholism is the invidious comparisons the emerging workaholic makes between himself and other people in the *amount of work* he is able to get done in contrast to others. Everybody knows how hard he works. He is the soloist. They are the accompanying choir in singing *his* song. He boasts about "doing more than my share," "carrying more than my part of the load." I can recall almost consciously making other men uncomfortable with the amount of work I was able to accomplish. The early signs of the workaholic syndrome are loud complaints in a line organization about other people's lack of conscientiousness. Ministers are particularly liable to do this because much of our work is of an unseen, intangible, invisible kind and we cannot point to specific results. Some of the most important things we do are things about which we cannot tell anyone. We feel uneasy about not having anything "to show" at the "show-and-tell" moments in the marketplace, such as at the meeting of the official board. Consequently, we are likely to spend considerable time discussing how busy we are, how much we have to do, and comparing the results of our "doing" with those of men we consider less productive than ourselves. If we are ministers, this is likely to show up in our efforts to produce tangible signs of our labors—larger numbers of converts, larger increases in membership, larger budgets this year than last year, the building of larger churches, et cetera. Of course, all this takes work, our work, and we never want others to forget it.

A third early tell-tale sign of the workaholic is the inability to say no to people who want to use his services, or to limit the time he will commit to other people. The professional person expresses this by taking on more speaking engagements, more committee chairmanships, more patients, clients, or counselees, more administrative responsibilities. He does not use time limitations, case load limitations, or the definition of his job responsibilities as his limitations. He is likely to feel the economic pinch but never knows at what point to level off his budget or how to live within that line. He always feels he must have more. However, subtle ego gratification is at work as well as economic anxiety. He feels that he is the *only* one who can do his work well. When challenged about whether he is overextending himself, he is likely to say: "But if I do not do this, who will?"

The wage earner, as differentiated from the self-employed and salaried person, will "moonlight" and add more and more to his load. For example, it is not unusual to find nurses who add on extra shifts to their regular hospital schedule. These wonderful persons are liable to become Florence Nightingales for their whole family and their in-laws as well, besides absorbing uncovered shifts in the routine of the hospital.

These attitudes are formed within the second and third decades of life when physical health and energy are at a high point. Never having known any limits on his health and energy, the person as a result tends to assume that there *are none*. The mood of omnipotence reigns. Yet, with a little attention at this stage of the game, possibly the person can be *taught* that there are limits. As one man said on the first interview of a longer-term counseling relationship, "I have always said that I will not stop until I am a $20,000 man." He worked a double shift six days a week. After the fifth interview, he remarked, "I am not a $20,000 man. I am a $10,000 man who works two shifts!" That was a beginning at least!

The Crucial Phase of Workaholism

The crucial phase of workaholism begins when the person's first collapse takes place. This collapse can be one involving interpersonal relations, such as when marriage and family life run into serious trouble. A young man tries to finish his last year of college, to earn as much as his wife even when this means working on a different shift from hers, and to beat off the draft by taking a heavy Army Reserve assignment; consequently, he and his wife have serious failures of communication. Or a staff physician takes so many private patients that he is asked by his hospital colleagues to resign. Or a prestigious young pastor has so many irons in the fire that he does not realize he is out of touch with his twelve-year-old son who has started using amphetamines, marijuana, and alcohol. These are interpersonal collapses. They call for a reordering of the life. They are trouble signals that call attention to the person's pathological preoccupation with work.

The crucial phase of workaholism may also be ushered in by a physical breakdown. A young university professor has a blackout and his condition is diagnosed as a propensity to low sugar content in the blood, rendered acute by improper diet and fatigue. A young social worker suffers a severe anxiety attack with associated physical symptoms over the impossibility of meeting the obligations of his crowded schedule. Such crucial situations precipitate the necessity for at least reappraising one's life plan, for defining more specifically one's goals, and the bases of one's motivation for work. A system of priorities must be developed. A new value structure must replace some old habit systems. But rarely does this happen. More often the work addict regards these crucial symptoms as something that will go away with a little rest. At the pleading of a spouse, the firm command of a doctor, and maybe a few words thrown in by a colleague who is himself a workaholic, he takes that little rest, but makes no basic changes in his life.

Chronic Workaholism or Rehabilitation?

After a crucial collapse or two the workaholic is at a crossroad of his pilgrimage, with no signposts. The workaholic can go in one of two directions: toward chronic workaholism or toward rehabilitation. The chronic case adopts his addiction as a way of life. He continues to let all other values go—family, friendships, spiritual associations, everything. He becomes an around-the-clock man whose whole life is his work. He eats, drinks, and sleeps his job. As William H. Whyte earlier described the organization man, so it can be said of the workaholic that he is an ascetic who enjoys nothing except an occasional good meal, constant supplies of work, and a good bed to fall into from sheer exhaustion. This goes on until death. Emotional responsibilities not related to his job are releated to other people so he can more easily fulfill his one all-consuming need for work.

If the person goes in the direction of rehabilitation,

however, new ways of life and value are opened to him. He redistributes his emotional investments into many different areas of life. He ceases putting all his emotional eggs in the one basket of work. The remainder of this book discusses the possible dimensions of these two approaches to the problem of workaholism.

II
Workaholics: This Land of Ours Has to Have Them

This land of ours is full of workaholics. The workaholic's way of life is considered in America to be at one and the same time (a) a religious virtue, (b) a form of patriotism, (c) the way to win friends and influence people, and (d) the way to be healthy, wealthy, and wise. Therefore, the workaholic, plagued though he be, is unlikely to change. Why? Because he is a sort of paragon of virtue. He is the one held up as an example by the little old ladies who tell boys and girls how to live. He is the one chosen as "the most likely to succeed."

The point of the discussion in this chapter is to identify ways in which the society or culture of which we are a part breeds more and more workaholics. Furthermore, the point is to suggest ways in which workaholism is the foundation of a way of life upon which much of American values are built. In a very real way this land of ours *must* have workaholics in order to survive as a culture.

Workaholism: A Collection of Religious Virtues

Workaholism is not necessarily synonymous with the Christian way of life. Let us hope not. There must be some better way of existing. However, modern popular religion has made the traits of the workaholic a sort of religious, although not a Christian, virtue. It would be better to say that workaholism is a collection of religious virtues that are open to reexamination in the light of the Christian faith in its unalloyed state.

The religious man today has two facets of his personality that tend to be taken to the extreme in workaholism. First, he is either successful or judges himself to be a sinner for not being successful. He has been captured by the prudential ethics of Orthodox Judaism and Puritanical Christianity which say that failure is a sign of sin, if not sin itself, and that success is a sign of virtue. If a person is rich and successful, then one is presumptuous indeed to raise the question as to whether he is really saved. If *he* is not saved, as the disciples queried the Lord Jesus Christ concerning the rich young man, who then *can* be saved? Poverty is a sure sign of cursedness. If the person were really trying, this line of argument goes, he would not be in the mess he is now in.

With such a moral world view, the work addict is confirmed in his ways. He has every justification for redoubling his effort each time he loses his sense of direction. *The* solution to any problem is trying harder and working more. If he has budgetary problems, the solution is to earn more money, not to reexamine the list of things that he wants. If he has problems with his family, the addition of work will both allow him to get away from his family and give him a pious reason for doing so. If they only appreciated him more, were not so extravagant, were not so lazy, and knew the importance of work, then the family would not have as many problems as it has. Furthermore, the workaholic cannot see the importance of *fellowship* at work. If a problem can be discussed with more privacy and relaxation at lunch, then let others take this less-than-Spartan way of working. The work addict would rather labor through lunch hour and eat a package of crackers and drink some milk or a soft drink! He is a success! Look *how* he becomes a success!

The second facet of today's religious man that can be taken to an extreme in workaholism is the need to have everyone's approval, at least outwardly. He does what he does in order to please people. This is sometimes called "service" by religious people. Consequently, the workaholic would rather say yes to demands made upon him than to run the risk of being rejected. He will promise anything just so you will like him. The end result is that he makes so many promises, he is overworked in fulfilling them. This is what David Riesman called "other-directedness," a kind of behavior determined from the outside rather than by an autonomous self that makes decisions on the basis of a carefully developed value system that has been thought through meditatively.

Such meditation in turn requires the development of an inner life. An inner life provides an inner-directedness that selects or chooses out of the demands made by others only what is consistent with one's own personal identity, rejecting and filtering out what is not consonant with one's real self. This element is missing in the workaholic. In seeking to please all others, he becomes overburdened and distraught and does not know who he is. One of the distinctly religious-psychological problems in work addiction is the loss of the sense of being a person in one's own right.

The element of contemplation itself that leads to inner-directedness is missing in the life of the workaholic. When I refer to contemplation, I do not mean the kind where one stares at the Maine coastline, nor do I mean the kind that requires a year's sabbatical to achieve. These circumstances may help, but they are hard to come by. Rather, by contemplation I mean that kind that is available to every man and woman. It is what Douglas Steere calls "the human birthright of all men, with no man excluded from contemplation by his unfavorable situation. . . . As man contemplates he is drawn to relate things."[1] The man or woman who contemplates draws back from the course of actions to ask about their total meaning, to ask who he is in relation to the course of action, and to rechart his course. He is like a driver who stops long enough to consult the map and check his location and direction. This the activistic, even "religious" workaholic rarely if ever does.

[1] *Work and Contemplation* (New York: Harper & Bros. 1957), p. 35.

Workaholism: The Organization Man's Necessity

The organizational life of business, industry, or the church tends to call for the workaholic. One asks whether this syndrome of effort-riddenness is not spawned by a bureaucratic culture. There are certain identifiable cultural factors in alcohol addiction and drug addiction which produce an "alcoholic culture" or a "drug culture," and my point here is that this is true of work addiction also. One kind of person that an organization must have is the man or woman who has *no* value that is not subordinated to the "good of the organization." He idolizes his outfit. If he celebrates his wedding anniversary, he feels he has to do it in such a way as to be good public relations for the organization. If he takes a vacation, it must be used in a way to make progress for the company, the school, or the plant.

Furthermore, this man does not work a given number of hours. He is always on call for the company. As William H. Whyte describes him and his kind, "they are never at leisure than when they are at leisure." This person is one who "is so completely involved in his work that he cannot distinguish between work and the rest of his life—and he is happy that he cannot."[2] This is rarely a salaried man who works so many days a month and year for his income, nor the nine-to-five man who when he finishes his daily stint forgets about work until his shift comes up again. This is a person who works around the clock. Let us take a look at his typical day.

He awakens at a specific time each morning without being called or without an alarm. He lies in bed for a few minutes and arranges in his mind every known detail of

[2] *The Organization Man* (Garden City, N.Y.: Doubleday, 1957), p. 164.

the schedule for that day. He ritualistically dresses and eats breakfast. He then moves through a day in which every moment is scheduled, except the time of leaving the office. At the end of the day—usually after everyone else has gone home—he never heads for home until he has gathered materials for work· at night. He eats his dinner, and his work is the main topic of conversation at the table. He then retreats to his workroom to make the best of the remaining hours of the day. He retires and spends the time just before he drops off to sleep in trying once again to solve the problems that defied solution during the day, rehearsing accounts of conflicts he has had with other people during the day, and experiencing considerable anxiety about the amount of work he has to do the next day, week, or month.

I recall a businessman telling me of an experience which changed his whole life. He decided that he was going to quit taking work home at night. He first did so by staying at the office until he finished, gradually reducing the length of time he stayed at the office. Then he disciplined himself to have all his work done by 5:30 P.M. He tells of the first evening he went home when the rest of the office force did. He stood outside the office building and watched each one go by on his way home. Then he went through an "almost physical agony" as he resisted the temptation to go back upstairs to work or to get his briefcase to take work home. He finally made a break for home and has neither worked late nor taken work home since.

My central point in this section is: the organization *needs* a few workaholics to prosper as an organization. Culture as we have it calls for this kind of devotee to his work—workaholics who live by a sweephand watch and dream of ways to give more time than twenty-four hours each day.

Workaholism in the Nine-to-Five Man

The impression I have left thus far would seem to suggest that the work addict is an upper-middle-class and lower-upper-class phenomenon. He is not. The recent concern about "law and order" has called attention to the wages of policemen and firemen. Because of their relatively low pay these persons are forced to take additional jobs as security policemen, night watchmen, fire wardens, etc., for private companies in order to supplement their income.

The same need is felt also by public school teachers, and even university and college professors. I recently found one schoolteacher who works in the evenings as a motel clerk, a job in which he could be paid extra and still have time to grade papers and prepare for classes the next day. During the Christmas holidays, he, being overweight, served as a Santa Claus in a nearby department store. These are persons with fixed-hour schedules who nevertheless moonlight in order to make additional money.

At first, the basic factor in overwork by people on fixed-schedule jobs seems to be purely financial. They need to make more money, which is not forthcoming from the public budgets out of which their initial salaries are paid. Usually they are in types of work where labor unions, and thus strikes for higher wages, etc., are taboo. Consequently the need for more income can only be met by taking extra work. On the surface, this seems to be *the* reason for moonlighting. However, closer inspection reveals other more subtle factors.

One of them is social prestige. These persons want their families to have what other families have, notably education. They and their wives both work in order to send their children to college. They themselves had to work long hours in order to get a college education. They do not want their sons and daughters to have to work as they did but to be able to give *all* their time to study. They want to have two cars so their wives can get around as they wish and so the children can have "wheels." They want to move to a better neighborhood so their children will have a chance to better themselves through the prestige of the kinds of friends they associate with, and marry.

As we probe underneath these social factors, we find the element of competition. In the Ten Commandments, we are told not to be covetous, but tradition approves all forms of competition. The ambiguous condition of the workaholic is that he works hard to get the things and the place in society that other men envy. At the same time he isolates himself from the very people whose approval he thinks he can get by outdoing them. The salty brine of competition is exciting to swim in, cooling to the skin as one revels in it, but does not satisfy the thirst for companionship and communion with others. As Samuel Johnson said in 1775, "That is the happiest conversation where there is no competition, no vanity, but a calm, quiet interchange of sentiments."

As we probe underneath the competitive factor, we find other causes of overwork. We find men who no longer can *see* the results of their labors. Even the assembly worker on the line does not *see* the total design of what he is doing. He has to assume that by doing his particular operation he has accomplished a great deal. The assembly line has removed the artisan from our culture; rarely today can one man in business for himself create enough pieces of furniture, jewelry, pottery, etc., to earn a living by direct sale of what he produces. There is a poignancy in the situation of a man who cannot invest his identity in the *substantive things he produces* rather than in the intangible of money. He has trouble communicating to his family the *worthwhileness* of what he is doing because he cannot show them the fruits of his hands except in the form of money. He cannot teach them his skill, but can only prove his manhood by bringing money home. It is little wonder that he seeks to work more and more in order to bring more and more money home. Yet all he gets as his reward is loneliness. Money creates a mythology of power in his family's mind; it also isolates him from them. He cannot easily teach his own children how to work or communicate with his wife about what *his* work is really like. Little wonder that he solves the problem by returning to work! When he is gone and at work, he feels that they understand a *little*. When he is at home with *nothing to do*, they have no place for him because they have organized their lives on the assumption of his absence.

Age and Workaholism

One of the things that our culture is doing for us and to us at the same time is enabling us to live longer. Even a full generation ago retirement for people of certain social classes was unknown. Social security has changed all this.

The middle-aged person approaching retirement begins to feel the pangs of his workaholism just when he has earned enough money to have the right to a certain amount of leisure because he doesn't know how to use that leisure. Also, unwillingness to spend money for recreational or creative purposes may actually express the fear of spending money without doing a sufficient amount of work to punish oneself for it. For example, one doctor told me that when he went on vacation he always borrowed the money because he would have to punish himself with work to pay it back, and this was just penance for the pleasure of not working!

The middle-aged person, furthermore, often feels the need to redouble his efforts in order to get ready for retirement. He continues to do repetitious tasks in order to have something in reserve for a "rainy day." He then may become severely depressed. Fortunately, excellent methods of treatment for "middle-aged depressions" are available, and a professional person can be of real assistance to someone who is suffering in this way. They have the "know-how" to help him decide things he hitherto has had no support in deciding. They can even intervene directly and decide a few things for him, such as specific changes in his work habits. Thus, although middle-aged depression is very painful, it can often lead the middle-aged work addict to do what he should have done in the first place without becoming depressed and feeling guilty about it: interrupt his routine of work, do something for a while that he really enjoys doing, and stop driving himself like a slave.

Today culture has created the possibility of more leisure time for us through a shorter work week. As a people, we have more of this world's goods at an earlier age. We are lengthening life; we can retire. Yet we have not escaped the compulsion about work that defies external efforts to make life easier. We have not found the answer to the covetousness that makes men compete with each other in their work all out of proportion to their needs. We have not found the secret of rest in the midst of plenty, renewal in the midst of work, and companionship in the atmosphere of loneliness that tarrying too long at the job produces. Our culture produces the workaholic. We need to attend to the nature of a society that needs such slaves to work, and at the same time to struggle against our individual compulsions to work.

The wisdom of the ages suggests that we must develop the contemplative life in the face of modern industry, bureaucracy, and technology. Several retreat centers are dedicated to developing this mood of meditation and contemplation. The Laity Lodge at Leakey, Texas, the Kirkridge Retreat at Stroudsburg, Pennsylvania, and others are examples. These contemplation or renewal centers offer comfortable accommodations with good food and good beds, in a restful natural environment of lakes and woods. The schedule is unhurried and permissive. A person's participation is not insisted upon. The retreat period extends over several nights, perhaps during a long weekend, or even disrupts the person's routine for a longer time. The leadership is usually skilled in the arts of meditation and relaxation as well as in understanding the psychological situation of adults. The stress is upon adult problems, patterns of living, and ways of renewal and revitalization of life. The program, which includes inspirational procedures, encourages dialogue between participants as they examine the order and disorder of their lives. Spouses often attend together and considerable attention is given to husband-wife and parent-child concerns. By definition, these retreats for the reexamination, refocusing, and redirection of the life of adults are a challenge to our culture, which tend to confirm rather than dissolve work addiction patterns. These tiny retreat centers are filled with people who paddle the little canoe of change up the stream of conformity to work addiction.

On the so-called secular side, we find that T-group (training group) sessions, interaction and sensitivity training, and the expansion of consciousness through natural stimuli have become a kind of therapy and renewal for harassed businessmen and professional persons. The increased happiness brought about by these techniques is a direct attack upon the isolation, compulsiveness, and rutlike existence of work addicts as I have described them here.

III
The Threatening Weekends

Eric Marshall and Stuart Hample compiled a group of children's sayings about God. One of them goes like this: "God made a lot of days so you wouldn't try to do everything at once."[1] The work addict, though, tries to get everything done every day. Time to spare is unknown to him. Therefore, the idea of a work-free weekend becomes a real threat to him.

This threat is real enough to produce a patterned reaction in many work addicts, one variously described by psychotherapists. Psychoanalyst Sandor Ferenczi, as early as 1918, gave his interpretation of what he called "the Sunday neurosis." He averred that "Sunday is the holiday of present-day civilized humanity" when "we are our own masters and feel ourselves free from all the fetters that the duties and compulsions of circumstances impose upon us." However, Ferenczi says, "it is not given to everyone to vent their holiday wantonness so freely and naturally."[2] Indeed, the neurotic attitude of the work addict actually causes him to suffer during his leisure time. Ferenczi speculates that his headaches, depressions, gastro-intestinal symptoms, may be caused by his fear of losing control completely of his temper, his sexual impulses. He may feel guilty about being free, and his neurosis both punishes him and incurs the punishment of others upon him.

Karl Abraham, another psychoanalyst, agrees with Ferenczi's estimate and contributes an additional insight. He says that "a considerable number of persons are able to protect themselves against the outbreak of serious neurotic phenomena only through intense work. . . . The mental balance which has been maintained with difficulty through working is overturned for the duration of a

---

[1] *God Is a Good Friend to Have* (New York: Simon & Schuster, 1969), p. 47.
[2] *The Psychoanalytic Reader* (New York: International Universities Press, 1948), I, 349 ff.

Sunday, a holiday, or possibly even for a longer period. When work begins again the patient immediately feels better."[3]

Abraham pushes the issue further in saying that because Sunday reminds people of the need to "enjoy themselves," it also reminds them of their inhibitions against any kind of enjoyment. Here is a clue that points toward a flaw in the total spiritual outlook of our culture which is focused in the institution of Sunday. It would be a revelation to look at our workaholic tendencies in the light of the meanings of Sunday, which are not all religious meanings by a long shot.

Sunday: Sunlight or Gloom?

We have considerable evidence to support the assumption that Sunday literally began as a day for the worship of the sun, an outgrowth of the deification and adoration of the sun in a farming culture. It was a massive admission by man that he is essentially a *dependent* person. To relax in the sun today, to participate in the fun of water sports in the sun, and to "go native" even in near nakedness is to revel in one's dependency. Sunday also thrusts us back into intimate involvement with family—wife, children, parents. Sunday involves us in our dependency upon them and theirs upon us.

The typical workaholic is as averse to admitting his dependent needs as is the alcoholic. As long as he has his work, he does not "need" anybody—he has power, place, and things. But when he shucks off the role of the self-sufficient one as he closes the office door or leaves the factory, he slams head-on into himself as the *dependent one*. Frequently, he is able to express this dependency only by developing physical symptoms which give him

[3] *Ibid.*

"permission" to be a child, to be cared for, fussed over, pampered. Without his being a "patient," few if any of his relatives or associates would perceive him as needing to be treated dependently. But, deeply, he like all human beings has strong dependency needs.

This points to the wisdom that the transactional analysts provide for us. They believe that each of us functions best when all of our three "ego states"—"the parents," "the adult," and "the child" in each of us—are permitted their appropriate times and places of expression. All three are *permissible,* and in need of wholesome affirmation. As a technically proficient person on his job, the workaholic makes decisions, accepts responsibility, and collaborates with others. This is his "adult ego state" at work. He is also a person whose "parent" state works overtime because even on the job "everybody brings his headaches to him." The playfulness and dependency to which he has a right do not have opportunity for expression until the weekend, but he has always denied these dimensions of his being and can permit them only when he is sick. Conversely, his family only knows to respond caringly to him when they see and hear "sickness" cues. Even his depressions are really "cries for love," as someone has aptly described them. If he could learn to put some of his needs into words—probably with some coaching from a therapist —he would be less likely to become sick or depressed or to be so gloomy and bored on weekends.

For even middle-aged persons can learn to play. Many workaholics are, as Sören Kierkegaard said of himself, like old men. Or, as an untutored grandmother said of me: "They put an old man's head on a young man's shoulders." To become as a child who can really play without inhibitions is a major spiritual discovery. I can recall one man who loved animals and pets but had never lived on a farm in his life. In middle age, after his children were grown and out of the home, he and his wife bought a small cattle ranch. In his leisure time, he revels in literally playing at what to other men would be work. Here is a man who at midlife is developing a whole new existence next to nature, and a whole new set of associates. He had been a "desk man" all his life; now he is a part-time outdoorsman. He has chosen sunlight rather than gloom.

Sunday: Creativity or Magic?

A second meaning Judeo-Christian civilization has given to Sunday is that of rest as a part of creation rather than as an interruption of it. Scripture tells us that "the heavens and the earth were finished, and all the host of them" in six days, "and on the seventh day God finished his work which he had done, and he rested on the seventh day from all his work which he had done. So God blessed the seventh day and hallowed it, because on it God rested from all his work which he had done in creation" (Genesis 2:1-4). Thus creation and rest are a part of the same act. The musician's "rest" is as much a part of the creation as his production of sounds.

A legend of John the Evangelist tells us that John was once playing with a partridge. Someone chided him for resting and enjoying the partridge in play rather than being busy at work. John answered: "I see you carry a bow. Why is it that you do not have it strung and ready for use?" He was told: "That would not do at all. If I kept it strung and ready for use, it would go lax and be good for nothing." "Then," said John, "do not wonder what I do."[4] This story makes graphic the truth about the role of rest itself in the economy of creation. Rest is not

[4] Robert Neale, *In Praise of Play* (New York: Harper & Row, 1970), p. 36.

just a diversion from labor but a necessary ingredient of genuinely creative work. For example, everyone can recall having at some point worked on a problem until the wee hours without success. Then, after forgetting about it for a time, resting, and even playing for a while, we came back to the problem and solved it easily. There is a point of diminishing returns in increased amounts of work. Quantitatively we may continue to produce, although even that is to be questioned. Qualitatively, however, our creativity inevitably diminishes.

But the question arises: if all that is said here is so obviously true, why do reasonable men and women become addicted to perpetual work? Robert Neale gives an excellent lead toward an answer: it is because we rely on the "magic" of our own clever efforts. He says that the spiritual creativity of life follows a pattern of "new discharge and new design." The response of faith and religion is one of rest and playfulness. I have shown this in the creative meaning of the Sabbath. Neale says that "magic is the work response" to the spiritual realm of life. By our own clever efforts and works, we seek to outwit our basic nature and that of the universe. Thus magic replaces creativity. The workaholic assumes that everything happens as a result of his efforts and therefore he must work incessantly. His attitude reminds us of that of the rooster, who proudly reminds God each day: "It is I whose crow causes the sun to rise!" With such vain fantasy, the workaholic becomes isolated and overloaded with a false sense of responsibility. "Nobody Knows the Troubles I've Seen" is his weekend theme. Effortless play and worship are replaced by the frenetic maneuvering of someone temporarily at a loss without his "work magic." His omnipotent fancies are shaken. The crucial psychological issue here is not, as Tillich put it, anxiety over one's finitude. It is buried resentment that we are temporarily frustrated in our imagination that we are gods, without the need for rest and renewal.

There are groups of workaholics who extend their magic efforts and strivings toward omnipotence into the weekend. Among them are the super-super-super-super church workers. I am not referring to persons who with a delightful sense of abandon enjoy the celebrations of their churches each Sunday. (They usually belong to churches where worship is not a duty, a work, or a merit-laid-up, but a spontaneously joyful celebration of the presence of God and the fellowship of each other.) Rather, I am talking of the person who goes at his church life as if it were another job in which by his unaided efforts the Kingdom has to be brought in before the sun goes down. These are church "slaves" who make those around them feel guilty if they, too, are not so enslaved. They are those who scour land and sea to make proselytes and then transform them into children of hell. They really are not very blessed people if that word means "happy" in the deepest meaning of happiness.

The Sabbath: Slavery or Freedom?

The Genesis stories of creation link the Sabbath to the creation itself. However, the Law links the Sabbath with the deliverance of the people of Israel from the bondage of slavery in Egypt. In doing so, the prophetic versions of the Law found in Deuteronomy link the Sabbath with social justice toward laborers in one's household. On the Sabbath, Deuteronomy 5:13a-14 says, "you shall not do any work, you, or your son, or your daughter, or your manservant, or your maidservant, or your ox, or your ass, or any of your cattle, or the sojourner who is within your gates, that your manservant and your maidservant may rest as well as you."

The motivation for this law is set forth very clearly. It is not the fear of God, nor the need to hew the line of ritualistic practice. Rather it is a motive of gratitude for deliverance from slavery, gratitude for the gift of freedom. "You shall remember that you were a servant in Egypt, and the Lord your God brought you up thence with a mighty hand and an outstretched arm, therefore, the Lord your God commanded you to keep the Sabbath day" (Deuteronomy 5:15).

The workaholic is a slave with no memory of deliverance from the rack of work. His esteem for himself must be constantly refurbished with tangible results of his own work—money, production figures, prestige awards, and various other trophy substitutes. These take the place of being loved for his own sake and thereby free to work or not work as the occasion calls for it. John Steinbeck put it well when he had one of his characters in *The Grapes of Wrath* say that if a man "needs a million acres to make him feel rich, and if he's poor in hisself, there ain't no million acres gonna make him feel rich, an' maybe he's disappointed that nothin' he can do'll make him feel rich."

If one feels loved securely for his own sake, this sets him free of the need to do things and to get things in order to feel worthy. But to do so, the love must be demonstrated. A hand must have been palpably outstretched. Sometimes this happens to a workaholic when a long illness takes hold of him and then lets him go. Sometimes it happens when the political situation of the place where he works gradually angles him into a position of a revered statesman. If this can happen prematurely and he can survive the transition without becoming disgusted, bitter, and soured on the world, he can indeed enter into a new psychological "promised land" without ever changing jobs. At other times, this deliverance takes place when a workaholic changes his place of work entirely and can start a new life in a new territory. However, somehow and some way, the workaholic must be *delivered* from the slavery of incessant work to the freedom of choosing to work when necessary and to rest and play freely when weekends and vacations come.

Such a deliverance stops the workaholic from being a slave driver toward those who work with and for him. He now can measure a man or woman's worth by criteria other than work, gauging it in terms of participation in play and rest as well. For example, how someone uses his weekends—albeit that this is his own private business—is as good an index to a fellow worker's creativity and freedom as the way he performs at the office during the week.

The part of the labor force in this country most prone to breaking the spirit of the Sabbath is the average minister. He tends to see himself as a lasting exception to the need for play and rest. He acts—and often speaks—as if the end of the world will come before he goes to bed at night, and all the work of God rests on his Atlas-like back alone. A comment I heard recently when speaking for a minister during his illness is illustrative. His main lay leader said about the pastor: "There's no doubt about Mr. X's consecration, but he does not seem to be able to agree with God that a day is only twenty-four hours long, and the week only has seven days in it. He's all the time trying to make this over on his own!"

The Lord's Day: Life Out of Death

The early Christians celebrated a "day of rest and gladness" once a week on "the first day of the week." They did so as a reminder that their Lord was resurrected on that day. To them the bondage from which they were set free was the fear of death itself. This fear is the master fear which prompts the workaholic to work compulsively. I have never met a work addict that I did not think was preoccupied subconsciously with the imminence of his own death. He works intensely, as if there is only a very little time left in which to accomplish his tasks. He runs the race of life as if the Grim Reaper were just behind him, gaining on him and aiming to cut him down all of a sudden.

Death is the symbol of ultimate impotence and finiteness to the workaholic. Work, on the other hand, assuages the feeling of impotence and demonstrates competence. It is to the work addict what sex is to the philanderer. The accomplishment of more and more work temporarily wards off the anxiety of death. However, when the weekend comes, and the defense of work is no longer available, the "Lord's Day" is a reminder of death and not a celebration of the renewal of life through resurrection.

I am using the idea of resurrection as a weekly event and not as a once-and-for-all, after-the-grave experience to be anticipated in the hereafter. Rather it is the continued renewal of life through the complete break with work in behalf of the new birth of a quite different way of life. As Boris Pasternak says, "During this brief interval of time, I shall, even before the Resurrection, attain my full stature."[5] This way of life means turning away from the drab Puritanism of work. It is a turning to the childlike grace of celebration, the quest for new experience, and the affirmation of the simplicities of life that are "givens" and not "earnings."

Resurrection, seen from this vantage point, is a within-this-life breakthrough into new dimensions of existence. It is not separated from the enjoyments of the body—rest, good food, sexual gratification, and bodily exercise.

[5] *Doctor Zhivago* (New York: The Modern Library, 1958), p. 557.

Rather, resurrection represents the union of all these basic functions of the body in the joy of life. Resurrection is the fulfillment and not the frustration of one's total being.

Hopefully, the weekend should and can mean just this to the workaholic. Once the other dimensions of life become worthwhile to him, he can be freed from being a one-dimensional man to whom everything is meaningless unless it is translatable into work.

One need not be a religious person to find the reality of the resurrection of life and defend himself from the death-dealing blows that labor in a technological world can inflict upon human beings. He has only to refocus his life on the creative use of weekends and evenings as a means of restoring the totality of life through rest, play, and making love. Then he has the beginnings of the wisdom on which the religious man's belief in the resurrection of Christ is founded. This cannot happen if the so-called gospel of work is taken as the royal way to salvation.

The point to all that has been said thus far in this chapter is that the work addict, whether religious or nonreligious, is only partly a man. The intended fullness and completeness of life is only available to him if he will consult the architectural design of human life in its totality. Included in the specifications are rest, play, and vital intimacy with people outside a work situation. There are definite ways of building these into a larger way of life, a completion of the design for human living. Let me suggest a few specific things to do:

First, admit that you are a workaholic and that you are powerless to do anything about it without help beyond yourself. This in effect is to admit your need for help from others. William Lynch is right when he says that "in our national culture there is a deep repression of the need for help. We dodge the fact that help is a part of the nature of hope. And we pay a price for such a repression."[6] This help may come from another work addict like yourself who joins you in the admission. It may come from your wife or husband, who may have been worried about you for years and never known that you thought anything was wrong. It may come from a son or daughter who has refused to be like you because they sensed something was missing in the example you were setting. The help may come from your physician who has faithfully recorded the effects of your intemperance in work upon your body. Or it may come from a pastoral counselor or psychiatrist whom you know and who has from time to time sensed with you your despair and loss of hope.

Second, make a fearless inventory of all the "busy-work" you do which is not really essential to or a real part of your job. Throw it overboard! Especially do so if it uses up your weekends and evenings. Also, do not make commitments to additional work assignments without (a) thinking about it overnight and (b) conferring with an-other associate, your wife, a trusted adviser-friend, or perhaps your nearly grown son or daughter who will greatly appreciate your confidence in his or her judgment.

Third, make a plan to spend a part of each weekend in meditation. This may or may not be in church. I am *not* making a pitch for church attendance here, for going to another meeting may be tantamount to going back to work! Rather, I am asking for a time for meditation. This means that you are either alone or with someone you do not have to entertain, talk to, or assume a role with. Meditation means that you systematically address your attention to the positive sources of strength in your life, whatever they are. You begin your meditation, therefore, with an exercise of gratitude for whatever forces in life have held you together thus far. You continue with an evaluation

[6] *Images of Hope* (New York: Mentor-Omega Books, 1965), p. 33.

of what really matters and does not matter in your life, casting aside that which does not really matter. Only you can decide what this is, but true meditation involves such a decision on your part. Finally, meditation involves reaching—reaching out of yourself to the companionship of others around you. This companionship must be based on *their* terms at first and then upon your reciprocal needs.

Fourth, remember something you greatly enjoyed doing when you were a teenager, and look for the chance to do it again. For example, one affluent, upper-middle-class man and his wife came from a small-town, semirural community in Appalachia where square dancing was much enjoyed. They took up this amusement again and are really revived by the time they spend at a square dance club. Another man liked to go camping with his father. His father is quite old now but he revived the custom himself and now takes his father camping.

Fifth, if you like to read at all, find something you do not have to read as a part of your job. It may be a mystery; it may be a novel; it may be the racing forms; it may even be the Bible. The important thing is that you do this freely and not as a form of slavery to the job. It could be that you are one of those latter-day workaholics who has come of age as a product of television. Add to your reading some television shows chosen because you like them and not to impress anyone on the job. If it is "Laugh-In" instead of something with snob appeal, so be it!

Finally, meet some new people you have not met before and renew contact with some old acquaintances with whom you have lost touch. The rat race of the average work addict's life throws him into deep relation with many people *for a time*. Some—not all—of these persons become steadfast and admired friends who do not require constant attention as the price for their friendship. It comes as a blessed surprise to them that you will have time for a telephone call, a home visit, or even a low-pressure social engagement. Then, too, new people in a community have fresh vitality to offer people who are tired of the same old faces, gripes, prejudices, and social groups. Meet three or four such people in a year, and then each weekend can be enjoyed for its own sake alone.

Other suggestions—especially with reference to a changed pattern of relationship to one's family—will emerge in the following chapters.

IV
The Wives of Workaholics

The particular collection of symptoms I have called workaholism is described by the Viennese psychiatrist Viktor Frankl as the "Executive's Disease." He says that in this disease "the frustrated will to meaning is vicariously compensated by the will to power. The professional work into which the executive plunges with such maniacal zest only appears to be an end in itself. Actually, it is a means to an end, that of self-stupefaction." In addition to not having "enough time for a breather or a meeting with himself, the executive fails to endow his wife's life with meaning." Therefore, Frankl says, "whereas executives have too much to do, their wives do not have enough to do. Least of all do they know what to do with themselves. . . . They flee from their inner void to cocktail parties, to gossipy social parties, and to bridge parties."[1] Often these wives become the victims of the stupefying effects of alcohol.

Male Work Addiction and Female Alcoholism

In the county where I live, especially in the more affluent sections of the city, it is estimated that there may be as many as eight thousand alcoholic housewives. In many cases their neighbors do not know that these women are alcoholic. About two hundred forty of the twelve hundred members in Alcoholics Anonymous in my county are women. A columnist in the women's section of the local paper calls this problem "the lonely disease."[2]

A case history of one of these women—so typical that it could be any one of them—gives some perspective on the situation of the workaholic's wife. Her husband is a fifty-five-year-old sales manager for a refining company.

[1] *Psychotherapy and Existentialism* (New York: Washington Square Press, 1967), p. 125.
[2] *Louisville Times,* January 7, 1970, Section B, p. 1.

He flies from one appointment to another in his private plane, leaving home late Sunday evenings and returning the next Saturday morning.

His wife is a forty-nine-year-old woman who submerged herself in the rearing of her children. But now the children are grown: a son twenty-six, another son twenty-three, and a daughter eighteen. The father's contact with the children has consisted of laying down the law, meting out punishment, and settling arguments when he comes home on Saturdays. The mother's emotional energies have been channeled into anxious management of every detail of her children's lives.

The adjustment held together with much strain until the first son married. He began to have severe financial difficulties, aggravated and complicated by a drug habit. His situation gradually deteriorated until psychiatric help was needed. He is now beginning the difficult task of liberation from his mother's overprotection and his father's rejection of him for being a "weakling."

In the middle of this crisis, shortly after the marriage of her second son, the mother revealed a rather longstanding drinking problem. After she made an attempt at suicide, the second son took the responsibility for having his mother temporarily hospitalized. The father's response to each of these crises was to fly back for twenty-four or forty-eight hours to "see how things were," then hurriedly to return to his work. The continuing responsibility for his wife has been left to her doctor, a minister, and the second son.

The second son became greatly concerned about the youngest child, his sister, to whom the daily task of caring for his mother was delegated by the father. This daughter, in her senior year of high school, is embarrassed by her mother's drinking problem, and survives by being apathetic about "the whole mess" until she can get away to college.

To complicate the mother's situation, her own mother and her only brother died within the space of a year.

The destructive nature of the interaction between this man and his wife is revealed in the way in which the sons and daughter are forced to pick up the tab for both the parents' unwillingness to make some clear decisions to alter their life patterns to fit the times of the middle years. A subtle fatalism in both of them whispers the message that they cannot change. Yet changes are taking place all around them, for which they are primarily responsible.

The father has a simplistic solution to this whole complicated mess: if his wife would just quit drinking, they would not have any problems! However, time is running out; his last child will be leaving home soon. This means that either he must change his work patterns in order to make his relationship to his wife a more sustaining one, or her present serious problem will become acute.

The Hyperactive Wife

The wife described above has taken the alcoholic route toward coping with the work addiction of her husband. Another coping device for wives of workaholics is to become absorbed in feverish activity of their own. Perhaps this is to say either that work addicts gravitate toward each other or that the addiction is contagious. Often marriages between workaholics were formed on the basis of the work being done. The young doctor, for example, marries a nurse or another doctor. The young minister marries an accomplished musician or a professionally trained church worker.

The workaholic wife is likely to echo one woman's statement, quoted in a remarkable survey of the marriages of "significant Americans": "Len brings home a bulging briefcase almost every night and more often than not the light is still on in his study after I retire. . . . My time is very full these days, with the Chairmanship of the Cancer Drive, and the Executive Board of the [state] P.T.A." Or, as a physician commented about his wife: "I'll bet if you talked with my wife, you wouldn't get any of that 'trapped housewife' stuff from her either. . . . She works as hard as I do."[3]

Work Addiction and the Budget of Life

At what era in a marriage is the relationship between a man and woman likely to be most critical if one or the other or both is addicted to work?

At different stages of our existence, we experience a critical shortage of different basic ingredients for survival. In a marriage, *money* is usually the critical survival factor when the couple is just getting started and when they begin raising children. As money becomes more plentiful, the budget of *time together* becomes critical. This may be the period at which the ingrained habits of addiction to work are formed. From a developmental point of view, the habits of this period are extended later into life when the realistic survival needs for money have been replaced by prestige and position needs. The person no longer works long hours seven days a week, twelve months a year, in order to make money with which to survive. He does so because he feels that he is indispensable, that no one else can do what he can do, and/or that he must get all the credit for the success of his organization or profession.

The worker now disregards the emergence of a different phase of life and the need for a different budget appropriate to it. He refuses to budget his *energy* as he

[3] John F. Cuber and Peggy B. Harroff, *The Significant Americans* (New York: Appleton-Century, 1965), pp. 52-53.

formerly budgeted money and time. When this happens, the person is normally in his late thirties to middle forties. He is in a crisis and can become an acute workaholic or set the stage for the addiction to become chronic. If he has a siege of bad luck at this time which does not hit his pocketbook too hard, he is likely to come to himself and to his senses. For example, if he is a politician and fails to be reelected; if he is an ecclesiastical worker and is not awarded some honor; if he is a senior executive in a company and the top position is given finally to someone else. All these are blows but not mortal ones. The individual retains his survival security, but "adornment security" is denied him. Thus, he is forced to come to terms with himself *as a person,* to make decisions about what is really important in life, and to reevaluate some of the aspirations that caused him to burn energy so recklessly.

Another set of circumstances that will tend to catalyze such reappraisal is an early illness—one that involves much pain, one that challenges the splurging of energy, one that even leaves the person with a mild handicap. In my own instance a fairly severe back injury in a softball game did it. I have seen heart attacks demand a reappraisal in other men. In women, I have observed a shift of values when they experienced a hysterectomy.

In the event that the "energy budget" does not precipitate a crisis, then two other budgets remain—the *communication budget* and the *work budget* itself. In a marriage, the communication budget is strained when all of the children are grown and leave the husband and wife alone. Howard and Charlotte Clinebell say that the children's leaving "itself often triggers the onset of the crisis and contributes to its severity. This is especially true in marriages in which spouses have used the children as a primary way of relating or as a means of avoiding intimacy (by always having the children between them as a buffer)."[4] Intimacy is an excellent word for a nourishing kind of communication. But unless intimacy is fostered and old habits dramatically challenged, then the next great crisis may be more than temporarily threatening to the person— it may demolish him.

The great crisis for the workaholic is retirement, when the budget of scarcity is *work itself,* not just those symbolic realities of money, time, energy, and communication it often represents. In the crisis of communication when the children grow up and leave home, a husband and wife may survive formally in their marriage by simply redoubling their efforts. They may, as the Clinebells say, quickly become "overinvolved in such things as their jobs, community services, and church activities, and eventually with their grandchildren. All these can be escapes from facing the emptiness of their marriage."[5] However, retirement makes it impossible to use work itself as a rationalization for avoiding the intimacy inherent in an optimum relationship to one's spouse. As Theodor Bovet says, "Marriage is subject to the same law as all living being: those who are unable to ripen grow old."[6]

Family Stress on the Family Vacation

The family vacation reshuffles the whole set of problems in the family interaction just described. It is essential to put the issue of vacations under a bright light in order to see their importance in the way of life of the work addict and his family.

[4] *The Intimate Marriage* (New York: Harper & Row, 1970), p. 125.
[5] *Ibid.*
[6] "The Middle Years of Marriage" (Paris: International Union of Family Organizations, June, 1962), p. 4. Quoted by the Clinebells, *ibid.*, p. 127.

When one examines the files of a good library on the subject of vacations, he is sorely disappointed. He reads that somehow vacations run against the grain of our whole culture, imbued as it is with the feeling that anything that is not work is somehow immoral. One reads in economic trade journals and business administration journals that the "fringe benefit" of vacation time is a burden administrators and management bear only at the behest of labor unions and of blue-collar, hourly-wage people.

The literature on vacations is even more telling when the larger problem of leisure is discussed. As Robert Calhoun says, technology "can reduce the amount of toil required of a given worker, but it cannot make him a whit more capable of the good life. . . . So long as he finds leisure only an occasion for unimaginative indolence, even a four-hour day will drag and vacations with pay will be boredom, as they now are for many wealthier folk.[7] These words of Calhoun, written in the middle of the Great Depression, were imbued with the idea of a vacation as a diversionary kind of pursuit other than one's job. Eugene A. Friedman and Robert Havighurst give a definition of meaningful leisure much like Calhoun's when they say that such leisure combines freedom from compulsion or "having to work" with the satisfactions found in work.[8] But Daniel Bell rightly queries: "If work is a daily turn around Ixion's wheel, can the intervening play be anything more than the restless moments before the next turn of the wheel?"[9]

We are dealing with this "slavery" aspect of work. The work addict *wants* to work because he *cannot* want otherwise. Havighurst misses the real meaning of the *compulsion* to work in his definition of leisure. The compulsive

[7] *God and the Common Life* (New York: Scribner's, 1935), p. 103.
[8] *The Meaning of Work and Retirement* (Chicago: University of Chicago Press, 1954), p. 192.
[9] *Work and Its Discontents* (Boston: Beacon Press, 1958), p. 37.

worker does not use his leisure because he is bound to that Ixion wheel of which Bell speaks. He *cannot want* otherwise.

Bell gives us a deeper motivation for enjoying leisure for its own sake. He says, "play may prove to be the sphere in which room is still left for the would-be autonomous man to reclaim his individual character from the pervasive demands of his social character." [10] Thus a vacation would be a time of withdrawal from the social self's demands and rediscovery of one's own personal space, one's private self, one's individual territory.

This would imply that a vacation might well mean freely and comfortably *doing nothing*. Sebastian De Grazia says that "perhaps you can judge the inner health of the land by its capacity to do nothing—to lie abed musing, to amble about aimlessly, to sit having a coffee—because whoever can do nothing, letting his thoughts go where they may, must be at peace with himself." [11]

A revered teacher and friend of mine became ill with a reactivated war wound. He was confined to his bed—which stands in front of a window that overlooks a large vista of the Ohio River—for several weeks. He was forced to do nothing but read. I took him a copy of Martin Buber's *I and Thou*. Buber's thoughts require considerable solitude, reflection, and leisure to appreciate fully. He wrote me a note in which he said that his illness had made him stop long enough to let his soul catch up with his body. Maybe this is what is happening when a person develops a "capacity to do nothing," as De Grazia says. Maybe this, in fact, is what the real purpose of a vacation is.

The first inside glimpse I got of another work addict's vacation was when my family and I took a two-month

[10] *Ibid.*
[11] *Of Time, Work and Leisure* (New York: Twentieth Century Fund, 1962), p. 341.

holiday in Europe between two lectures I had to give, one in England in May and another in Germany in early August. We were spending a week in a beautiful old hotel facing the beach at Nice, France. We met another family who had daughters the same ages as our sons, as well as one older daughter. The mother said to us about her husband, who was ill: "He is a businessman and his business is his life. We come here for two weeks each year from our home in Holland. The first day we are here he is worried about what he forgot to do in his business before he left. He makes telephone calls to attend to this. The second days he eats too much and becomes sick at his stomach. The third and fourth days he spends in bed. Then he begins to surface." When asked what "surface" meant she said: "All year he is submerged in his work. When we go on vacation he starts coming up from under it. He seems to get the bends. If we can help him survive the first week, he enjoys most of the second week, but toward the end, he becomes preoccupied with all the work facing him when he returns to the office."

This woman seems to be an expert in the care and feeding of work addicts! She and her daughters nevertheless were able to enjoy the beach. And although they were close with each other, they also extended their companionship to us as a family. It was here that I began to reassess my own attitude toward life. I had nothing to do—there were no telephones, I had no speeches to make, no one knew me in my working roles as teacher, minister, and pastoral counselor. When they responded to me, they responded to *me,* not my position or responsibility. I had time to muse to myself, to amble about aimlessly, to sit in a cafe and drink coffee, to let my thoughts go where they might, to be at peace with myself, to get acquainted with myself.

This leads to my own positive definition of a vacation: A vacation is any set of circumstances that takes you out of your accustomed official roles. A teacher such as myself is constantly before groups and crowds as a speaker and leader. This is a working role. Right now, as I am writing this, I have no speaking engagements and refuse to take any. Being "out of my role" has many of the characteristics of a good vacation. However, I am still in a working role as a writer, and to that extent not fully on vacation. I enjoy this as work twice as much because it is the only one of my several working roles I have to fulfill. It is almost like a vacation to be able to do only *one* of these things at a time.

Getting out of one's working roles enables a person to experience his own individuality more fully. He is less programmed by other people's social cues and expectations. He can be who he is in that moment, then and there. He can refuse to treat the "now" as full of demanding antecedents or as a means toward some future end, and instead can enjoy it for its own sake. As Bertrand Russell says, "The modern man thinks that everything ought to be done for the sake of something else, not for its own sake."

Today has been both work and vacation. I have been to the library, which classifies as work since it was done not for the sheer enjoyment of wandering and wondering— that would be a real vacation from work—but in order to complete this chapter. But when I met two preschool girls from a church group who were collecting Betty Crocker Cake Mix coupons for a kidney machine for use by indigent patients and brought them home to my wife to negotiate this transaction, *that* was sheer enjoyment because it happened unexpectedly and was wholly in the *now*. As such, that part of my day was vacation. And when I took my wife out to dinner and got her out of her accustomed role of cooking and caring, she had something of a vacation too.

Another characteristic of a vacation is that you get out of the position of being a means to other people's ends. The usual day's work is taken up in being and doing what is useful to other people. This is perfectly appropriate to a *working* way of life. Even our Lord Jesus Christ said, "I must work the works of Him who sent me, while it is day; night comes when no man can work." He said this as he healed a blind man. He was a means to this man's ends—voluntarily. But a vacation is a time when we exist as people in our own right and, not as a means to other people's ends.

This conception of vacation focuses the fallacy of using a vacation to visit relatives *if* these relatives demand you use the visit as an opportunity to settle grievances between them or engage in home-style psychotherapy, or if they require you to play familiar work roles, as when a woman is forced to spend time in the kitchen helping to prepare elaborate meals for large numbers of people. People returning exhausted and depressed from such safaris are right when they sigh: "That was no vacation!"

Yet, if relationships are good and the time unfettered, a visit to one's homeplace is a real vacation to many people. They do some of the things they did when they were children—boating on a river, swimming in a lake, lying under a shade tree after eating at midday—or enjoy simple pleasures like sleeping without a telephone beside the bed. One doctor I know would return to his homestead at a time during the fall when the leaves were changing colors. He spent his days wandering in the woods and his evenings reading before an open fire. He slept twelve uninterrupted hours a night. His mother let him do all these things without comment or criticism. She fixed him food she knew he liked. He was a boy again and nobody objected.

He spent these vacations without his wife and children, who came to understand that he needed such a complete change and who worked out a way for the entire family to have a vacation together as well: this year he took an additional week's vacation with them at the beach. Then they played together as a family, and he and his wife each shared with the other the things they individually most enjoyed. He liked to go deep-sea fishing; she liked to play bingo; they did these things together. But most of their time was absorbed in being a means to the children's happiness, doing what they wanted to do.

So during a third week in the year, this same doctor and his wife went—just the two of them—to New York. They renewed their sexual play with each other in the "delicious naughtiness" of their hotel room. On Wednesday and Saturday afternoon and two evenings they went to plays. On one or two days they "got lost" from each other; she went shopping and he went to bookstores and bars. (The small town in southern Kentucky in which they live and work has neither elegant shops, bookstores, nor bars!)

I mention details from this man's private life as a possible answer to the dilemma of vacations for the normally over-worked, self-employed person. The doctor's pattern is not the only one, but his vacations, as all good ones should be, are tailor-made for him rather than bought off wholesale racks. Furthermore, they reflect consideration for, without submitting to domination by, his mother, his wife, and his children.

In Summary: Some Plain Suggestions

The work addict does well to number his days and get himself a heart of wisdom, as the Psalmist says. In plainer language, he needs to find out what time it is in his life as a whole and to wise up. It is later than he thinks. He may find useful a few plain suggestions for a life inventory. Here they are:

First, arrange an appointment with a specialist in internal medicine for a thorough examination—cardiovascular, gastro-intestinal, genito-urinary, muscular-skeletal, ear-nose-throat, and pulmonary. The examination should also include an interview in which work, play, and marital habits are discussed. It should involve a frank discussion of your moods of depression and lack of energy as well as your moods of elation and splurging of energy. The question of food and drink intake in relation to your energy needs will require close inspection, as will your eating and exercise habits. Inevitably this will focus on the workaholic's use of food to ward off fatigue and to allay anxiety in fixation upon work. Sugar intake, for example, in the form of sweets or alcohol gives quick energy, usually at the cost of extra weight!

If you choose a wise doctor whose own way of life you admire, you are likely to establish communication at a confidential level that you very much need. This is a wholesome first step for the work addict to take. It is such an important step that larger companies in some instances are establishing their own routines of medical service to accomplish the same thing. There is no real substitute, however, for a completely private consultation with a personal physician.

Second, become involved in a group of persons of your own age and station in life who are solving these and similar problems of work. It is better if you can do so along with your wife in a couples' group. This can be done at a variety of levels and in differing contexts. For example, if both of you have a weight problem, you could consider "Weight Watchers" groups and the use of the same health club facilities. If you are active in a country club, you might get a professionally trained psychologist or psychiatrist to form an "Adjustments of Life" or "Growth" group that meets regularly. If you belong to a church, you may be surprised to see how well trained your minister is in leading small group sessions in personal growth and problem solving. If you do not belong to such community fellowship agencies, then the psychology department of a local college, university, or theological seminary may well have the personnel needed to establish a group counseling pattern in which you can participate.

Finally, reevaluate the whole economy, pattern, procedure, and purpose of the *vacation*. Arrange a holiday that changes your *role* in life, even if it is temporary. A group of research people in a study of vacations outlined the following elements which experienced vacationers identified as important:

1. *Freedom from programming by other people or too much preplanning by oneself.* This pronounces the "death knell" for those kinds of *work* devoted to programming other people's vacations for them.

2. *Release from customary norms of conduct.* This should be a welcome suggestion for those who enjoy getting out of the confines of conventional rules.

3. *Getting away from home, especially if it is an unhappy home.* This explains some teen-agers' desire to go on a journey by themselves to be free of parental conflict.

4. *New experience.* This speaks to the monotony of the daily grind. Meeting new people, changing one's mode of living from urban to rural, from small town to huge city, from an academic setting to a fishing village, from a landbound to a waterbound environment, etc.

5. *Going from a perfectly safe experience to one that has the possibility of danger.* This explains why my sons enjoy scuba diving, why some senators enjoy mountain climbing, why some people take up stock-car racing as a hobby, etc.

With the contemporary two-day weekend (an invention of the last few years), the pattern of official holidays, and the two-week to one-month vacation, the typical work year today looks something like this:

    104 weekend days
      7 special holidays
     14 vacation days
    125
     16 extra days in the event of one-month vacations
    141
    224 working days
    365 days a year [12]

The workaholic is living in an unreal world if he does not face up to the reality that one out of every three days is available for the meaningful use of leisure. While he should not tactically schedule every moment of leisure, he should have a conscious overall strategy that *he* has chosen. He should exercise his freedom from slavery by deciding for himself what the interruptions of work can mean. The crucial problem in the use of leisure is that the person has to decide for himself how to use his time. At work, it is usually decided *for* him. In this respect leisure calls for more independence than does work. It calls for more initiative and creativity. The work addict retreats into work rather than confront the insecurities and risks to be met in the world of play, repose, and unprogrammed contact with life itself.

[12] George A. Lundberg, Merra Komarovsky, Mary Alice McInervy, "The Amounts and Uses of Leisure," in *Mass Leisure,* ed. Eric Larrabee and Rolf Meyerson (Glencoe, Ill.: Free Press, 1958), pp. 173-98.

V
The Sons and Daughters of Workaholics

The first real questioning of my own defective pattern of work occurred on a Saturday. Our elder son—then four and a half years old—and I were building a work bench for his toys in the basement. The time came for me to go to my office to meet a counselee. He became sullenly angry and said bluntly: "If you didn't have to make so many appointments with these slopheads, you and I could get our things done!"

The message did not really get through to me, however, until about a year later. We were living in New York. I was teaching in the summer session at Union Theological Seminary. At that time this same son asked for an *appointment* with me in my office. He said that he had a "problem" he wanted to talk about. I asked him if we could not talk about it then and there. He said no and insisted on an appointment. I arranged a specific time and, to my surprise, he arrived on time at my office. The problem he wanted to discuss was the Resurrection—how could this really happen and what is Jesus like "right now"? I told him that this was a thing we do not exactly know. We can know from Jesus' earthly life, however, that he must be really wonderful. Also, we are told in the Scripture that when we see him finally we will see him as he is because we ourselves will be like him. This is the promise I like to remember. He said he would like to talk with me some more sometime and asked if I were ready to go home. We enjoyed a slow walk back home together.

From this rather sobering experience, I learned that I had scheduled time for everyone except my own sons. From then until now I have used the ritual of making specific times with our two sons. Sometimes this is hard to do because they, too, have taken on some of the hyperactivity of their father. However, it does accentuate one truism about the role of children in our lives: their life of play can save us from working ourselves to death. Children's interruptions of whatever kind, in fact, are the "hallowed times" for the person who senses that they are unique, nonrepetitive moments. Therefore, practically all else can wait. The great moments in their lives—their first dates, their getting a driver's license, their graduations, their inductions into military service, their returns from war, their weddings, their first permanent jobs, their children's births—these are nonrepetitive events that take priority over all other commitments. But more than this: just being there when an issue of character is to be decided, a question of a broken heart is facing them, or the like, is the main challenge to the work addict's misplaced sense of values. For his presence and wholehearted attention, there are no effective substitutes. Missing these moments is the rather heavy price the work addict pays to be "a significant American."

Young People Speak

Consultation with several young persons about the attitudes of their parents toward work has revealed some valuable insights:

First, they said that the main characteristic of a work-addicted parent is his or her *preoccupation*. With one accord they said that the parent always has "something else" on his mind.

A second factor was *haste*. One said: "You never see him. That does not mean he is never there. It just means that he is moving so fast you have to look twice to see him going by!"

A third factor these young persons mentioned was *irritability*. They seemed to know that their parents were so deeply involved in their work that it made them cross and irritable. They seemed to perceive that their parents' irritability derived not so much from anger at *them* as from being "bugged" by their jobs. The youngsters felt that their work-addicted parents took work too seriously, lacked humor about the whole process.

This relates to a fourth factor mentioned by the young people about their parents' overcommitment to work: *depression*. The children were *aware* that their parents were depressed about their work. They were concerned that their parents could not work and be happy as well.

These characteristics are symptoms—real and apparent to the young person. We need understanding of the background of work addiction and this collection of symptoms. When queried as to *why* their parents would be preoccupied, hasty, irritable, and depressed about their work, the same young persons formulated *three* sets of dynamics.

A Background of Poverty

The first set of dynamics they identified as the work addict's early experience of poverty. Many work addicts went to work very early—some as young as six or seven but ordinarily in the early teens. They never really had an adolescence. They worked in order to eat; they never learned to play. These parents habitually say: "When *I* was your age, I was earning my own living!" Although the survival problem is long past, the absence of play—a habit never learned—is still operative.

I myself am familiar with this set of dynamics. I went to work as a page in the United States Senate when I was thirteen years old and went to high school in my spare time. I supported myself from that time forward, and *never* had to borrow money from anyone until I was a twenty-two-year-old senior in college and needed a pair of glasses. My pride lay in not asking nor owing anyone for anything.

Deeply embedded in this independence was a driving sense of competition to "show up" the sons of wealthy and educated families who were also pages in the Senate and later fellow students in college. The drive to work was powered by what I have chosen to call "the proud inferiorities" of the poor and disinherited.

All of this was, in my case and that of millions of others, aided and abetted by the Great Depression. Today's middle-aged workaholic is very frequently the person who as a late teen-ager (I "retired" as a Senate page at seventeen) had to walk the streets and beg for a day's work in order to eat. The parents of teen-agers like myself in that era *could not* themselves be workaholics—they were more often than not unemployed! But they taught their sons and daughters to overvalue their jobs. And in turn those children are middle-aged workaholics now, who still have the habit of over-commitment to work.

Today the sons and daughters of these affluent over-workers represent a strange "return of the repressed," manifesting the need of their parents for a time of playfulness in their lives. Some of these young people wear clothes and have haircuts exactly like their parents *had* to wear when they walked the streets looking for work during the Depression—unbarbered heads, and worn, even dirty clothes. These young people *ask* to live as simply as their parents who had no choice in the matter!

The Affluent's Drive Toward Success

My young informants' second estimate of the roots of workaholism arises out of their own experience with both their parents and their peers. They point out that many of their friends in school work and study all the time. They cannot be satisfied with good or even excellent grades. They must have *perfect* ones—because their affluent parents *drive* them to succeed. One of these young women told her mother that she did not believe that her mother wanted her, the daughter, to make perfect grades for her own sake but because of what it did for the mother herself. Her mother was somewhat taken aback, but owing to the excellent program of personal therapy she and her daughter were engaged in, she could affirm her daughter's wisdom and admit that it was so.

Another young person said that he believed that getting good grades was a reasonable goal. However, he said that life involved more than grades and that school was not the only place he could learn what he needed to know. Yet he pointed to friends of his whose parents insist they be forever at their studies or using all of their leisure time to do something directly contributive to success at school. A college student, for example, majoring in fine arts, is forced by his parents into additional arts as a pastime. My informant's judgment was that getting good grades is often the price a young person pays for the love of his parents—a love experienced, however, as being not for him but for the trophies he brings home.

Another young man in his senior year of high school was deeply devoted to a young woman also in her last year, but he couldn't get a date with her because of the busy schedule her mother had programmed for her. They tried hard to find some time to be together, but he finally gave up in despair because, he said, he did not have a chance against the girl's programming mother. It needs to be said that this young man was a serious student himself, not a dropout, "goof-off," or "acid head." He felt that the girl should have *some* times during the week not scheduled by her mother. So they broke up their courtship. The crucial issue was the girl's having "some free time and the right to decide how to use it." This is an example of the second set of dynamics, those springing out of the affluent family.

The Social Class Treadmill

My informants pointed me to a third set of dynamics: the *aspirations* of people who work in order to progress up the social ladder. They push their children unmercifully, not in order for the children to go to college, but in order for them to go to a *prestige* college. Going to school is not enough; one must go to the most exclusive school with a droppable name. These young persons are ordinarily "second generation" college students, children of parents who were the first ones in their families to go beyond high school. The parents had become work-addicted by working and going to school with no financial backing from their families. Often they went to school over their parents' objections and certainly without their parents' approval.

Now, under the guise of "wanting their children to have it easier than they did," they insist that *their* sons and/or daughters must have the *best* education and have all their time free to study. Underneath this attitude, however, lies a denial of their own heritage and an attempt to correct their own past by means of their sons and daughters, through whom they can deny their poor and ignorant forebears.

The material symbols of social advancement are another source of overwork. They cost money, either drawn from established sources of income or earned by taking on additional work. Men who returned from World War II and the Korean War, for example, felt "behind" educationally and economically. With vast bursts of energy they worked overtime at one job or added another job to catch up on the things they had missed. This was a cause of parental workaholism which the young people overlooked. A draftee tends to regard military service as a miserable interruption of life which must be made up if he is to "get ahead" in life. People moved from the one-car affluence of a post-

Depression era to the two-car affluence of a postwar era. Today's high school and college students are frequently the victims of the *three*-car thrust, possibly even of the push toward ownership of *two* homes, one in the city and one in the country! Of course, this applies to the so-called "leisure class," who in fact are not at leisure at all. The fathers and sometimes the mothers are working overtime to pay for the symbols of success—houses, cars, boats, campers, and *prestige* education—which their children may appreciate but for which they pay a psychological price.

Lewis Sherrill, in his book *The Struggle of the Soul,*[1] says that too many people's lives are repetitious, monotonous treadmills. The social class cycle of getting *things* as symbols of "getting ahead" is a treadmill that never stops turning. It is another version of the Ixion wheel. The necessity of working more and more in order to keep the wheel turning is one of the driving factors that produce workaholics. As Wordsworth says:

> The world is too much with us; late and soon,
> Getting and spending, we lay waste our powers:
> Little we see in Nature that is ours;
> We have given our hearts away, a sordid boon!
> This Sea that bares her bosom to the moon;
> The winds that will be howling at all hours,
> And are up-gathered now like sleeping flowers;
> For this, for everything, we are out of tune;
> It moves us not.—Great God! I'd rather be
> A pagan suckled in a creed outworn,
> So might I, standing on this pleasant lea,
> Have glimpses that would make me less forlorn;
> Have sight of Proteus rising from the sea,
> Or hear old Triton blow his wreathed horn.

It would indeed be a deliverance from the treadmill of "getting and spending" to have some contemplative time

[1] (New York: Macmillan, 1951.)

by the sea, as Wordsworth describes. But, maybe the secret of wanting to work less rests in reducing the number and expense of things which must be bought. Can old things be renewed? Maybe one way of diverting our energies from the job to other activity is a hobby in the repair of things to avoid buying new ones. Thus, maybe one would save enough money to finance a modest trip to the seaside. Then he would have both time and money to stand on the pleasant lea and have glimpses that would make him less forlorn!

The Hobby and the Workaholic's Children

Recently, I asked a large class of mine to write their own spiritual autobiographies. The central characters in these dramatic stories were the students' parents. One of the most vivid differences among the students (now in their early and middle twenties) was that some could recall vivid, positive memories of sharing activities with their parents whereas others had no such memories. The latter group spoke of how fatigued, how worried, how irritable, and how basically unhappy their parents were. This was not ordinarily said in recrimination of their parents but with a sort of helplessness as to what they—the sons or daughters —could do to change their parents' lot to a more restful, carefree, relaxed, and happy one.

The *kinds* of shared activities in the first group ranged from the standard hunting, fishing, camping, and traveling together to less expected ones like sharing a business trip with a father, going to town from the farm on Saturday afternoon for a movie and ice cream, going berry-hunting together, and making homemade wine together.

As I explore my own relationship to my sons, I recall those rare occasions when I have gone along when they scuba-dive; when I have helped build a darkroom for our youngest one who loves photography; when I have taken them and their mother with me on long work assignments out of the city; and when we have more recently worked on various vintages of automobiles together.

I suppose parents of daughters would have different stories to tell. For example, making one's own clothes seems to bring great satisfaction to daughters whose mothers have taught them the skill. Older, married daughters seem greatly excited in talking about cooking special recipes. Some daughters take up their father's hobbies. For example, I know one young woman whose father taught her how to fly a plane!

The typical workaholic looks on these kinds of activities as interruptions of his work. He is likely to feel that they are things he endures in the "now" until work resumes. To quote Bertrand Russell again, "Everything is done for the sake of something else and not for its own sake."

This points to the work addict's criticism of his or her sons or daughters as always playing, never looking ahead, not planning for the future. It seems that the measure of pain in these judgments is due to the parents' extreme attachment to overwork producing an extreme disdain for work in the youths. After all, if they recognize work as the cause of their parents' unhappiness, why should they choose to be like them?

I feel that a compromise can be developed between the adult work addict and the young children and adolescents in the home. Whereas the vacation is a model form for tailoring a better husband-wife relationship, the hobby or the *avocation* is the model form for tailoring a better parent-child relationship. The father, particularly, can learn much from his sons and daughters. Margaret Mead, in her book *Culture and Commitment: A Study of the Generation Gap*,[2] says that there are three types of relationships between parents and children. The first is postfigura-

[2] (Garden City, N.Y.: Doubleday, 1970.)

tive, in which the old are models and examples for the young. The second is cofigurative, in which the peer group becomes the model and example for the young. The third is prefigurative, in which the children become the model for their parents who must learn from the child how to alter adult behavior. In reality all three of these types of relationships should be at work simultaneously in a creative family.

When it comes to avocations, the workaholic is almost forced into the third pattern of relationship—learning from his sons and daughters how to change his adult behavior. The real test of character is: is he open to it, and can he sit still for it? I say that he can do so and that it can be fun. Young people can teach their parents camping skills they learned in summer camp while their father sweated it out in the office. They can share their enthusiasm for fixing and working on old cars. They can take him swimming with them. They can show him how to sail. These can be "openers" to get him loosened up enough to *want* to do something apart from the daily grind.

If a workaholic is not in good health, he needs a more sedentary kind of learning of the uses of leisure. He and his wife may have used television merely as a babysitter in earlier years, not realizing that they were helping to create a "postliterate world" in which young persons tend to learn through visual and audio media rather than through books. The children now can teach the work-addicted father what purely diversionary excitement certain programs on television can bring. My sons have a definite routine for my joining them to watch the fascinating underwater documentaries of Jacques Yves Cousteau. Also, other parents tell me how their sons and daughters have started them to going to movies again to see such things as *A Man for All Seasons, The Pink Panther, The Graduate,* or one of Ingmar Bergman's films. Rarely do these young persons and their parents go to these movies together. Rather each goes with his or her own peer group, and the family shares the experience by talking about the film at home, after a meal, or late at night. The film often opens up lines of communication between the generations in a quite unexpected manner. The effect on the workaholic parent is salutary because now he feels less alone, more understood, more affirmed.

As the workaholic becomes gradually accustomed to the idea that play is sensible, he may have his courage strengthened enough to launch out on his own. He begins actively to search for diversions from his work. I remember one particularly early routine I used. Instead of having a business appointment at lunch, I decided to go alone to a new restaurant as often as I could. I would slip away from the job and the crowd and go to a strange part of the city. I still do this. Just the other day I discovered a little unpretentious German restaurant that has superb food. When I find a good place, I occasionally take my wife there to dinner, or take a visiting colleague or a daily associate with me for leisurely, uninterrupted conversation.

Other writers offer some very helpful suggestions about diversionary or "hobby" types of activity. Robert Calhoun says that several criteria should be used in choosing such activities.[3] First, he says, the activity should give you "a chance to learn." He suggests behavior that would enable you to learn about your neighbor and his job. Another criterion, says Calhoun, is to choose something that puts us into closer touch with nature. I have a colleague whose pet dog diverts him from overactivity. He almost copies some of the dog's ways. Lin Yutang says that man is "the only working animal. With the exception of a few draught horses or buffaloes to work a mill, even domestic pets don't have to work. Police dogs are but rarely called upon to do their duty; a house dog supposed to watch a house plays most of the time, and takes a good nap in the morning

[3] *God and the Common Life*, pp. 103-4.

whenever there is a good, warm sunshine." [4] We do well to get in touch with the world of animals, whatever this means to a particular individual. One man raises chihuahuas as a hobby; another man enters Siamese cats in a pedigreed cat show; another man has a covey of prize pigeons.

The interaction of a person with plants is another way of getting in touch with nature. We receive each year an invitation to visit the iris garden of an English teacher in a local college. Another busy pastor surprised me when he showed me the orchids he grows. A bachelor in the Deep South used to own and operate a pecan grove. He was quite eccentric about selling them. He would advertise in the paper: PECANS. FOR SALE AT TOP PRICES OR FREE. SUIT YOURSELF. He did not have to sell them and was glad to share them with people. However, if they insisted on making money off him by buying large quantities for resale, he wanted top prices! This is reminiscent of Robert Frost's attitude toward pines and spruce being used for Christmas trees. The point of his poem is that he would rather give his trees away lovingly one at a time as he met and came to know those who wanted them than to sell them by the thousands to some "city guy" who would only pay him a nickel apiece for them.

Speaking from a religious point of view, American religion has been much too utilitarian to include the world of plants and animals in the scheme of value. But the Eastern Orthodox religion has. Some Far Eastern religions have carried this to the extreme of deifying animals. However, one can profit by extending the reality of meaningful life to *include* plants and animals. They slow our pace, challenge our dependence upon our own efforts, and teach the art of cooperation with, rather than antagonism toward, nature. It was the Founder of the Christian faith who said: "Consider the lilies of the field, how they grow; they neither

[4] *The Importance of Living* (New York: John Day, 1937), p. 145.

toil nor spin; yet I tell you, even Solomon in all his glory was not arrayed like one of these" (Matthew 6:28).

Let us return to our major subject in this chapter—the children of workaholics. In a seminar on drug abuse and use which a colleague and I taught in the spring of 1970, we were able to have two young men who were actively on drugs—marijuana and LSD—visit the class as guests. At one point they said the reason they took drugs was to "find a cool place for their heads." The "heating up" of consciousness in the overstimulation of competition is the way of life the work addict provides for his sons and daughters. As Calhoun says, if a person can use his leisure to get in touch with and learn from nature—along with those whom he has fathered—I am convinced that drugs for both him and them will cease to be necessary.

A third criterion for choosing an avocation or a hobby is drawn from the behavioral therapists. They claim that work addiction is a "wrongheaded" set of conditioned, or learned, behaviors. Such behavior can be unlearned and better modes of behavior substituted. Therefore, their suggestion is that a person should take up some amusement for which he has a natural taste, however limited. Then they would say to act energetically *as if* this were intensely enjoyable. Their theory is that the *feeling* will follow the *action* and not vice versa. Then the new habit is established.

I have discovered that this is true of beach life. We live a long way from the seashore. The mammoth effort that it takes to get there requires about three days of acting *as if* this were a major and enjoyable project. Then as the grip of the sea takes hold of me, I no longer have to push myself. I gladly do nothing; I wander aimlessly; I enjoy not working. The job seems distant, unreal, and unwelcome. But I can recall the time that I did such stupid things as scheduling graduate student supervisory conferences while I was at the beach!

VI
The Workaholic on the Job

No real evaluation of the workaholic's way of life and how to change it is possible until we analyze the man actually at his job. An internal view of the workaholic in action, where he is reputed to be happiest, is necessary for a full understanding of work addiction.

Major Types of Workaholics

Previously we have been talking about *one* kind of workaholic, the dyed-in-the-wool kind. Careful observation of a business organization, a hospital staff, the military, a church organization, or a school reveals a *variety* of different types of workaholics. Therefore, we must describe and classify these various types.

The Dyed-in-the-Wool Workaholic

This man or woman has several characteristics as you see him or her in action on the job. First, whatever kind of skill and/or profession he practices, *he is a "professional" at it.* He takes the standards of excellent performance more than seriously; these are well nigh his total personal ethical code, if not tantamount to a religion for him. He will not touch an assignment lightly or halfway. To him there is no such thing as giving an assignment "a lick and a promise." He leaves his own professional stamp on a job if he accepts responsibility for it at all. A noncompulsive professional will be able to settle for a less than perfect result. The workaholic *has* to get 100 percent results.

Already you are beginning to see that the dyed-in-the-wool workaholic is a real *perfectionist*. He is merciless in his demands upon himself for thoroughness, mastery, and peak performance. Every operation for a workaholic physician is a dramatic, command performance. Every transaction of a businessman workaholic must be meticulously planned, forcefully accomplished, and followed up for a specific appraisal of the results. The workaholic minister is impeccable in his preparation and delivery of sermons and performs over and above pastoral service to people in distress. The work-addicted salesman will feel double pride in taking care of his personal customers, accounts, and so on.

Another characteristic of this kind of work addict is his *vigorous intolerance of incompetence* in those who work with him. His relationships with his fellow workers will be cordial, relaxed, and even warm until someone starts blundering—according to his estimate. Then the workaholic is hard, even impossible, to live with at all. He is apparently without qualms as to the consequences of telling off both high and low if he thinks they are doing a sloppy job.

This perfectionism and corresponding intolerance creates a parallel relationship to the peer group of the workaholic and to his superiors, or the authority structure. The peer group tends to isolate the workaholic because of his unquestioned competence which makes them feel that he is in a class to himself. Yet, when the real dirty work has to be done, they elect him to do it. They hate his guts but know that he will get the grimier jobs done. For example, he is an ideal candidate to become a union steward. He often is the unofficial and unpaid ombudsman for the organization. Because of his "eccentricity credit"—i.e., his earned right to be different, due to sheer accomplishment, and because of his job security and aggressiveness—his peers say "let him do it." All of them may consider themselves as Moses, appointed to the supreme leadership, but they think of the work addict as Aaron who does their talking for them when the going gets rough. In these conditions lie some clues for breaking the power of work addiction.

On the other hand, the executives feel ambivalent about the workaholic. They *need* him when a program is to be put into action. Yet they fear him. Their authority is an imputed, constituted, official authority. In the long run it has the last word. But they fear the workaholic because his authority is more personal, functional, and earned. In the day-to-day operation of the plant, the company, the school, or the church, the workaholic's presence must always be taken into account in many major and minor decisions. A project can be adopted on paper, but it is the workaholic who must translate it into a working, day-to-day, functional reality. In most organizations there is quite a collection of these workaholics. The typical administrator is ambivalent toward them because they are both a blessing and a problem to him. They are a blessing because they get the job done; they are a problem because they have the prestige to buck the boss with some impunity.

A fourth characteristic of the dyed-in-the-wool workaholic is his *overcommitment* to the institution, business, or organization for which he works. I have often speculated that some men and women replace their fathers, mothers, or siblings with the institutions they work for. It is not by chance, for example, that a school is called *alma mater,* "our mother." This unconscious cathexis or attachment to a particular institution is the drive shaft of work addiction. I have had an opportunity to study this, since I have collaborated with a number of institutional physicians as they made decisions to change jobs. Their primary commitment was to their profession as doctors, in which they always had the option of private practice as a way of making a living. By contrast, I as a teacher have always had a keen sense of institutional commitment; and prior to the painful reappraisal of my own addiction to work, I was overcommitted to the institutions and organizations I was affiliated with. They became the be-all and end-all of happiness to me. This led to considerable unnecessary distress, for I could not distinguish between simple loyalty and compulsive overcommitment to an institution. Andras Angyal is exceptionally helpful here. As a person moves from a pattern of unhealth to one of health, Angyal says, he "can gain a new life only by losing his life as a neurotic. . . . He is assailed by many doubts. . . . If I worry less and drive myself less, shall I become lethargic, lose my ambition, and end as a bum?" [1] But it takes a leap of faith to "let go." The institution is *not* a person, and its life or death does not depend on the anxiety of any one individual.

This discussion of overcommitment is clarified by comparison of the adult workaholic's situation with what Kenneth Keniston calls *un*committedness on the part of alienated youths. He studied what he called "the alienation syndrome" in a group of thirty-six Harvard students. He argues that their alienation is an extreme reaction to "dilemmas of upbringing, to social stresses, and to historical losses that affect their entire generation." One thing was certain: these youths looked upon the world of their parents' social order as a "closed room with a rat race going on in the middle. . . . They expect little in the way of personal fulfillment, growth or creativity from their future roles in the public world." They were "cool": which "means above all detachment, lack of emotion, absence of deep commitment, not being enthusiastic *or* rejecting of adulthood." [2]

A final characteristic of the dyed-in-the-wool workaholic is that he usually is both talented to begin with and has acquired a set of highly marketable skills. He is much in demand. If he has no effective internal way of rating his priorities, he is likely to take on more and more over and

[1] *Neurosis and Treatment* (New York: John Wiley & Sons, 1965), p. 240.
[2] *The Uncommitted* (New York: Harcourt, Brace & World, 1965), pp. 18, 397.

above his prescribed activities. Thus he collides with himself in the face of the many demands laid upon him: he is a perfectionist but he commits himself to so many people for the use of his skills that he cannot do his job well. This results in an anxiety depression amounting to panic. His sleep is more and more curtailed by the sheer problems of scheduling and by his effort to prepare for his responsibilities when he should be sleeping. The morass of contradictory demands is too deep for him to extricate himself from, and something has to be done by others to rescue him. His life has become unmanageable.

The Converted Workaholic

A second type of workaholic is the arrested or converted workaholic. He comes from the population just described. He is a "professional," but he has taken seriously the nonprofessional's way of life. The professional man is by nature a round-the-clock man. The nonprofessional is, if he is a farmer, a "sunup-to-sundown" man; if he is an industrial or white-collar nonprofessional, he is a "seven-to-three" or "nine-to-five" man. Also, these nonprofessionals guard their free time jealously. If they use some of it, they have to be paid time and a half; if they work very much overtime, they have to be paid double time.

Therefore, the professional who is a converted workaholic requires exceptional pay when people make his five-day week into a seven-, eight-, or nine-day one—but he will do the extra work if paid for it. Also, for the normal day's work, he sets a hypothetical limit and stays within it. For example, it took several illnesses for my body to get the message through to my brain that I was a compulsive worker. Once it did, I decided that I would not travel past midnight, that I would not accept engagements that required my participation morning, afternoon, *and* evening in any one day. I decided that I would go to work at a specific time each day and come home at a specific time.

Earlier than this, as I've described, my sons had taught me that Saturdays were ours, and I ceased to make Saturday and Sunday appointments. Today, as a professional teacher, lecturer, and writer, it is a regression to workaholism for me to take evening or weekend work assignments. I know that I have offended some of the people with whom I work in a large religious organization by confining my work day to sunup-to-sundown. If I get roped in on additional assignments, you may be sure I was napping, not looking, or at least knew better!

The converted workaholic is a person who "lets each man prove his own work," to quote the Apostle Paul. He confesses his intolerance and repents. Several motives can prompt such a change: the energy required in fretting and fuming over other people's failure to function is wasted because this does not even occasionally change their behavior; the feeling of responsibility for other people's performance is unrealistic, because each person has to prove his own work and "every tub has to sit on its own bottom"; and it is sheer arrogance to assume that you and I are *the* judges of what competence is in another person.

As a work addict turns himself around in ways I have suggested, he begins—much to his surprise—to enjoy more approval from his peers and his superiors. They feel less intimidated by him. He senses that his *work* is not what wins their approval. If he does not work quite so much they like him better. Strange, but true.

This suggests that the quiet strategy the converted workaholic should adopt is to defer to someone else when extra work (for which there is no extra pay) is about to be loaded upon him. If this is impossible, he can use the occasion to identify problems in the line organization that make it unwise to accept the extra work! This will mean that the powers-that-be will be on one level convinced that he is not as reliable as they had first thought and on a deeper level relieved that they are now free to choose a less threatening man for the job. If he succeeds in avoiding extra work, the work addict has only one more hurdle to get over. He has yet to go home and tell his wife that he has refused the extra work. Some wives do not see it as extra work; they see it as extra prestige! This kind of wife helps make both alcoholics and/or workaholics, depending on the degree of piety in the family. Happy indeed is the man who, when he comes in and announces to his wife that he has refused a prestige assignment because it involved extra work and no extra pay, is greeted by affirmation, approval, and even a kiss!

If, despite all efforts, the extra work cannot be refused for any of the reasons above, another reason is at hand for the man whose character has changed enough to say no at all costs. He best defends himself when he goes back to the *basic satisfactions* of his job. If he is a commercial artist or an architect, he simply says: "I cannot do that because it would take me away from the drawing boards and that is where the company makes its money." If he is a salesman, he refuses to take a desk job at the maximum salary of his commissions. He says: "I can't be happy unless I am closing sales contracts." If he is a teacher, he refuses a department chairmanship because he would be distracted from giving his undivided attention to students. This has been the most valuable discovery for me. I get my basic satisfaction in classroom work, in writing, and in individual counseling of students. Other assignments tend to fret, distract, and preoccupy me. In explaining this to my colleagues, my superiors, and my family, I find understanding and appreciation from all of them. This is the singlehearted way of approaching the problem—all competitive, manipulative, and remunerative considerations laid aside. In fact, the best way of dealing with overcommitment to an institution is to limit your commitment to the main reasons that you chose to be there in the first place.

As I have said, the dyed-in-the-wool workaholic has a set of highly marketable skills. Therefore, he is in great demand. If he is a converted workaholic, his problem is in limiting the extra demand that moonlighting opportunities create. The basic income and standard of living of the man and his family has much to do with this. Later, when I discuss the situational workaholic, many variables will be mentioned about this particular factor. However, I am writing on the assumption that the semi-self-employed person is being provided for at an above-subsistence level by his company, school, church, or organization. Moonlighting functions as "over-and-above" work for "over-and-above" benefits. (Often the working wife's salary is for these purposes.) A couple should, therefore, put a ceiling on the amount of money actually required—including compensation for inflation—to cover wants over-and-above necessities. Then the *number* and *kind* of additional work assignments can be chosen accordingly. For example, I have decided to earn only "X" number of dollars by additional work assignments and take per month only that much work.

This sounds simple enough, but it is not that easy. Men and women sometimes take extra work for prestige reasons. A doctor chooses to work six months in a prestigious clinic as an expert in a particular procedure, teaching it to that staff. A professor is called as a consultant on a new project for a government agency or another nation. A minister is asked to do a national television series for his denomination. Too often these jobs pay off in honor, prestige, publicity, with money a secondary consideration.

We might conclude that it is men's egos—not overwork—that kills them!

The element of omnipotence sneaks into the workaholic's thinking. He fantasizes that *he* is the *only* person who can respond to these requests. If for any reason he turns such an opportunity down, however, he may discover that he was fifth or sixth on the list! And if he waits and observes news notices, he will certainly discover that other people followed him on the list. This should teach the work addict the lesson that came to me as good news: I could save myself a lot of additional work if I declined the opportunity and recommended another person. I learned this from an older pastor when I was visiting in his office. While I was there, the phone rang. The call was obviously from someone inviting him to take an important engagement. He declined graciously and said: "Whereas I cannot do this, I wonder if I might mention Mr. X., a new pastor in our state. I know him to be a very competent man for such an opportunity!" Go, and do likewise!

The Situational Workaholic

We come now to the person who is new on his job, is in the "starvation period" of his profession, or is at the lowest pay echelons in his organization. This man overworks out of real necessity, not for inner psychic reasons, not for prestige reasons. He may have reasonable job security but large amounts of economic anxiety. It is not a part of this person's basic personality to work incessantly. As his practice becomes established or when his salary rises to a more adequate level, he corrects his course easily and lives more sensibly, letting work recede to a normal place in his value system. Nonetheless, he is a candidate for compulsive work addiction. The prestige system of his organization or profession, the prestige needs of his wife, the kind of neighborhood he lives in all serve to determine his habits. Not the least significant factor is the kind of older colleagues he has as advisers and models for his behavior. Younger men tend to pattern their standards of living, work habits, and approach to life on older professionals. Administrators of schools, hospitals, churches, and professional societies seem to be unaware of this element in their work patterns.

Sometimes the situational workaholic is a person whose job security is minimal. He may be new in a company that has periodic layoffs, and the last to come is the first to go. He may be in a trial period with his organization, such as under three-year nontenure contract on a university faculty. In overperforming to achieve security, he is often preparing the inner ground for compulsive overwork later on.

The Pseudo Workaholic

A fourth type of workaholic is one who has many of the characteristics of a true dyed-in-the-wool workaholic, but these are superficial. They are specific competitive accommodations to the pecking order of the organization. This person does his work in order to move from one echelon in the power structure to another. His orientation to work is not a production orientation, as in the case of the dyed-in-the-wool workaholic; his is a power orientation. He does all the right things to ensure promotion. These include having a very active social life which obligates the "right people" to reciprocate his hospitality. It involves doing favors in abundance for power figures in the organization. Thus the pattern of "I've scratched your back, now scratch mine" is set in motion. The focus of interest in choosing things to do on the job is to follow the in group. If the in group is thrust out of power for any reason, he shifts, without apparent embarrassment over the inconsistency, to the new in group although their position and function on major issues is diametrically opposed. This cannot be understood unless it is seen that this man responds consistently to power and not to issues. He is opportunistic in this respect, but can be counted on to respond this way.

The pseudo workaholic may be spotted by the lack of perfectionism in his work. He makes many brilliant starts in what he does, but when the prestige of having made a dazzling beginning wears off, the long pull of the carry-through is odious to him. He is likely to leave one project for another very soon. The pseudo workaholic changes jobs often. He is strictly an image man, not a performance man. Laurence Peter and Raymond Hull state it well when they say *"an ounce of image is worth a pound of performance."* [3]

The real commitment of the pseudo workaholic is to the prestige and power the organization offers *him*. He draws his name *from* the institution; he does not give his name *to* the institution. The institution is strictly a means and in no sense an end in itself. There is no attachment to or affection for the organization. In psychoanalytic jargon, the pseudo workaholic is narcissistic. As Browning said of one of his characters, this person is deeply in love with himself and probably will win the match!

The pseudo workaholic, furthermore, moves vigorously and actively until he reaches the limits of the prestige system. Then his real character emerges. He is basically a playboy who, as Laurence Peter and Raymond Hull say, has been promoted *beyond* the level of his competence and *to* the level of his *in*competence! These men, in their painfully humorous book, lay bare the "Peter Principle" that

[3] *The Peter Principle* (New York: Bantam Books, 1969), p. 121.

"for each individual, for *you,* for *me,* the final promotion is from a level of competence to a level of incompetence." [4] The real work "is accomplished by those who have not yet reached their level of incompetence." [5]

I never really found a better explanation than the Peter Principle of a phenomenon I have seen monotonously in educational institutions. Assistant and associate professors carry the burden of the work of the institution (what they themselves do not pan off onto instructors, that is). As one university professor put it, "a *full* professor is one who is *gone full-time.*" I have noticed the way in which full professors tend to move in four or five different directions. Some become involved in consultantships, outside lectureships, etc. Some become feverishly concerned with campaigning for a position in the administration of the school. Some become totally absorbed in their hobbies—golf, raising bird dogs, game roosters, horses, etc.—to the neglect of their job. Some become full-time invalids, preoccupied with health problems. True, some focus hard on teaching. They are the real oddballs!

These are ways of saying that the pseudo workaholic is a more populous breed than the dyed-in-the-wool workaholic.

The Escapist Posing as a Workaholic

I would not be true to the facts in describing the different types of workaholics if I did not make note of a very common phenomenon: the person who simply stays on the job—or in the place of work—rather than go home. I noticed this first when I was a page in the United States Senate and discovered there were a few senators who slept in their offices regularly! I will admit that this is extreme, but in a variety of organizations in which I have worked

[4] *Ibid.,* p. 8.
[5] *Ibid.,* p. 10.

and in a large number of those I have observed, this species of worker exists, even if there are but few of them. A chaotic marriage is the cause for some of these situations. The marriage in which in-laws live in the home is another. I saw one case in which *both* sets of in-laws lived in the home. In other instances, the worker simply enjoyed the company of the people he worked with more than he did that of the people at home. For this person work was a substitute home.

Occasionally, I have seen single persons make the real mistake of expecting their job to substitute for *all* other relationships. Of course, we have a whole subculture of persons in the Roman Catholic Church who operate on this as an articulate, ordered set of values. But when it occurs without such cultural support and institutional moorings, the effects can be very frustrating, unsatisfying, and confusing.

These persons are not, ordinarily, workaholics in the sense of being compulsive workers. For them work is an escape, and this is very different from a compulsion.

Some Guiding Principles on the Job

It is one thing to curse the power-and-light company, and another to light a candle. I think it is time to light a candle. I have done my share of the other. Some principles of health for a group of workers in a bureaucratic situation are as follows:

First, a man or woman should fear like a plague the fate of being given a new position that calls for skills in which he is not interested, for which he has not been trained, and which do not afford him basic job satisfaction. The usual reason for going into such work is not ordinarily financial. Rather it is prestige and power. These are like salt water. Salt water does all the things fresh water does—it is wet and cool, it washes, etc.—except the one thing we need water most to do—quench thirst. Power without work satisfaction is the same: it just makes you want more.

Second, the man on the job should decide what he can best do and do it with singleminded devotion. A devout people would call this being at peace in the intention of God for our lives. Regardless of what one's image in other people's eyes may be, this should be what he strives for.

Third, health in relation to work may require that the worker reappraise his family relationships and decide that he is going to exercise leadership in his own home. An ancient Christian source suggests, for example, that the person who accepts a position of responsibility in the church must first have demonstrated effective leadership in his own home. The worker cannot continue to be intimidated by the prestige needs and money drives of his wife and children. He must lead them.

Fourth, the worker needs to begin developing a sense of humor if he does not already have one. The rollicking sense of humor with which Laurence Peter and Raymond Hull tell in a serious jest about how incompetency in an organization rises, like cream, to the top, and there sours, is a wholesome example of what I mean.

VII
The Woman Workaholic

All that has been said previously tacitly implies that workaholism is a uniquely masculine malady. For years, the same mythology enshrouded the alcoholic. I want to do away with the misconceptions concerning the problem of work addiction in the lives of modern women. The temptation of an author who is a man is to assume that the problem is the same for both sexes. I want to challenge this assumption and to describe some of the unique problems of women with work addictions.

I have pointed out that there are dyed-in-the-wool workaholics, situational workaholics, pseudo workaholics, and escapist workaholics. Generally speaking, these categories may be applied to women. However, the special effects of feminine psychology and of the different cultural demands placed on women call for separate treatment.

The New Situation of the Working Woman

The typical and expected role for women in our society is as wives and mothers, and it is coming to be recognized how much unpaid labor is involved in these functions. At the same time, the proportion of women in the paid labor force has been rising: between March 1960 and March 1965 it rose from 30.5 to 34.7 percent. By 1968, 41.6 percent of females over the age of ten were working, and made up 35.5 percent of the total working population. Thus when we consider the woman at work, we must think of the *work addict in the home,* the *work addict on the job,* and furthermore the *work addict in the community and church,* since women have customarily played important roles in these arenas, too. All three may be dimensions of the same woman's life, and there may be significant interplay between them. The complexity of the situation is suggested by the results of one study of married working women: the more tradition-oriented the women's view of marriage was, the happier they were, and the more modern-oriented, the less happiness they experienced. In addition, the orientation of the women was greatly influenced by the amount of education of the husband.[1] Since the wife-and-mother role seems so influential in women's attitudes, we begin by observing the woman workaholic in the home.

The Workaholic Woman in the Home

The Fear of Pregnancy and Work Addiction

It is common for young couples not to want to have children for a while. The young wife is likely to say she wants to work first, to use her training. Yet, as the years accumulate and no children come, such women become panicky, lest they may never be able to have children at all. Medical examinations of the wife and husband reveal no physiological reason for their childlessness. Psychological evaluations, however, often uncover the wife's unconscious desire to hold on to her work. She may have a deep wish to keep her independence; or she may genuinely want children, but profoundly distrust her husband's ability to earn a living for the two of them and their child. Or she may feel that in becoming pregnant she will be failing to fulfill the expectations of her parents, who educated her to become a professional woman. Or she may have renounced her own professional ambitions in getting married and now continues to work in order that her own educational ambitions may be realized through further graduate work by her husband, with her financial help. Thus she works around the clock—both to assuage

[1] D. K. Kotelman and L. D. Barnett, "Work Orientations of Urban, Middle Class, Married Women," *Journal of Marriage and the Family*, February, 1968, pp. 80-88.

her frustration about not having children *and* to accomplish her more superficial ambitions.

The Compulsive Childbearer

When someone named childbirth "labor," they rightly identified it as one of the most exhausting types of work there is. Childbearing, too, can be a compulsive kind of work. Helene Deutsch, a psychoanalyst, speaks of "compulsive motherhood" in those women who "try to achieve the full experience of motherhood by begetting a new child again and again." [2] These women repeatedly become pregnant but miss the fullest sense of motherhood. Deutsch suggests some of the unconscious factors operative in compulsive motherhood: the mother may feel guilty and not be able to enjoy sexual relations apart from impregnation; she may be unhappy with any kind of baby except a new, helpless one; she may sense in pregnancy a way of controlling her husband and the other children by being the center of the family; she may see childbirth as punishment for being a woman and thus constantly use it to punish herself and atone for being who she is.[3]

The end result, regardless of motive, is the martyred wife and mother; and the condition of the compulsive mother is overwork. The work addiction of the compulsive childbearer has many of the characteristics shown by the dyed-in-the-wool workaholic—perfectionism, desire for mastery and control, considerable depression, etc.

Such a person needs, more than other compulsive workers, intensive counseling, and her husband's role may require professional attention as well. A family service organization, one of a whole national network of such

[2] *The Psychology of Women*, Vol. II: *Motherhood* (New York: Grune and Stratton, 1945), p. 269.
[3] *Ibid.*, p. 327.

counseling agencies, could be of genuine assistance to such a woman. There is a double reason for such help: the mother in her own right has more happiness in store for her than she knows; and having children for other motives than the love of the child itself creates unwanted and unloved children who not only suffer pain themselves but may become social problems. The primary consideration, however, is the mother's basic privilege of happiness and effectiveness as a person; it is in that light that both her marriage and her motherhood must come up for review. She has a right to be "delivered" herself rather than to be always "delivering"!

The Workaholic Housewife

"Man's work is from sun to sun, but a woman's work is never done." The proverb reflects the common assumption that the housewife must always be at her chores. With the invention of labor-saving devices—clothes-washers and dryers, automatic ovens, dishwashers, vacuum cleaners, refrigerators, "instant" foods, precooked meals, garbage disposals, disposable diapers, etc.—considerable quantities of housework have been converted into the need for more money to pay for these services. This has enabled and required more work outside the home, frequently by both partners.[4]

Even the housewife who does not work outside the home finds that all these conveniences have simply shifted the arena of her work rather than diminishing it. She spends

---

[4] What follows is a description of the middle- or upper-class housewife. Usually wives in lower-class families have to work *outside* the home. The care of the home itself in these instances is handled by a grandmother, by a babysitter, or by an older son or daughter, especially when there are younger children to be cared for. The presence of a woman in the home as a full-time mother and housewife is increasingly a luxury today.

much of her time negotiating with repair people to keep gadgets in working order. She spends a large portion of her day chauffeuring around her family, who a generation ago would have walked or used public transportation or car pools. With the telephone in the home, she spends considerable amounts of time sending and receiving messages. She is the "control tower" operator of a home that is more like an airport than a private abode. Everybody lands and departs on schedules which require almost computer-like mastery of detail to synchronize.

If the housewife is a part of a home that operates as I have described here, she is also the custodian of charge accounts and checking accounts. This in itself calls for infinite patience and attention to detail. The apportionment of this responsibility varies from home to home. In many instances it takes all the acumen both the husband and wife have to give.

Add to this the responsibilities for entertainment, both personal and official. The protocol involved requires extensive detail work—telephoning, scheduling, and weighing relationships and interactions in a company, a school, a church, or a governmental structure in which she and/or her husband are involved.

Under the circumstances described, the housewife often becomes addicted to her housework to the neglect of other values. Some observations about her patterns of behavior and a few of the reasons behind them are in order.

The workaholic housewife is an example of perpetual motion. Her favorite phrase is: "Let me do it." When a visiting friend, relative, or passing stranger says "May I do that?" she firmly says "No," and means it. She generally spurns domestic help, insisting adamantly that she would rather do it herself. She, too, is a perfectionist. No one can do her work right but herself. If her husband, knowing that she has a big luncheon for the wives of the departmental staff, makes the beds for her before he leaves, for example, she is likely to do the job over or correct it!

Her perfectionism means she cannot teach her sons and daughters how to wait on themselves, care for their own rooms, and in general learn the skills of caring for a home. Yet she often expresses martyr feelings for having to "clean up after everybody's mess." She will fuss but she will not command and she will not teach. This is particularly disastrous in her relationship to her daughters, who often grow up without knowing how to cook, sew, clean, and decorate in a home.

Again, the work-addicted housewife may have an unsynchronized schedule. She may be just the reverse of the "computer-like" housewife. She may either go to bed later than the rest of the family or arise very much earlier than they do. If she does, she makes a great deal of this and remonstrates with her family for needing so much sleep.

Furthermore, the workaholic housewife has a compulsive sense of cleanliness and order. She rarely makes a place where children can be messy, as they tend naturally to be. The *house* is an end in itself, and not simply the environment for bringing children joyfully through each stage of their growth. So identified is such a woman with her house that any injury to it is taken as a *personal* offense, and may be felt almost as damage to her own physical appearance!

Why such compulsiveness? Several reasons come to mind. The workaholic housewife may well have been the oldest child in her family, or the only daughter in a house full of brothers. Consequently, she might have been burdened very early with the care of the house. Possibly her mother worked outside the home, and controlled the home through the daughter. The daughter was accepted or rejected, and love given or withheld, in terms of the way she kept the house. Little boys—or tom-boy girls—were her sworn enemies, because her relationship to her mother stood or fell on whether the house was well or poorly kept. Thus "the house" became her territory, and to transgress against the house was to threaten the very basis of her security.

Another suggestion as to why the housewife is work-addicted rests in her inadequate handling of aggression and anger in the face of frustration. This tends to produce a situational kind of workaholism, which is nevertheless very real. For example, a middle-aged woman's husband was dying of cancer. It was a long, slow process, punctuated by periodic hospitalizations. During this time, she arranged for, had built, and moved into a new house. She would arise at three or four in the morning and turn a set of yard lights on so she could work with the landscaping, the flowers, the shrubs, etc. Her yard is a showplace now, five years later. When her husband finally died, she ceased this pattern of work. Her anger and distress were expressed. She faced her frustration in the finality of grief rather than trying to overcome it through work.

Women who are unusually "sweet," always smile, and never express any anger verbally have a way of becoming addicted to work. They approach their housework in the tradition of the woman pictured on cans of Old Dutch Cleanser, who runs with upraised stick as if to chase and beat the dirt! One of these saccharine but driven persons visited our home recently, and engaged our seventeen-year-old son in a thirty-minute conversation. When she left, he said: "O.K., gang, let's all rest our faces from grinning now!"

Another force behind the work addiction of the housewife is her substitution of activity for conversation. As long as she is busy she does not have to talk. In fact, one of her recurrent phrases is: "Can't you see that I'm busy?" This may be native inarticulateness, or it may be an escapist kind of behavior. She does not *want* to get into discussion with her husband or her children. Children are to be seen and not heard, and husbands are to be avoided. Her custom of keeping late hours may have developed to avoid sexual contact with her husband but, even more, to avoid bedroom conversation of an intimate nature. Even sexual activity itself may be used to avoid conversation, and be experienced as a form of *work* she has to get done, another chore to check off her list of the duties of the day.

The avoidance of communication through work is to some extent a way of avoiding intimacy in all human relationships. It becomes most excruciating, however, in the husband-wife relationship, which demands or creates the expectancy for more intimacy than any other. In this context, a housewife's work addiction may be both an escape from intimate conversation and a nonverbal expression of withheld affection and indirect anger toward the husband.

Finally, however, a housewife's work addiction may be a reaction to work addiction in her husband. She would gladly stop her work and go to a play, or out to dinner, or swimming, or on a brief holiday. But *he* has this, this, this, and that to do. She feels playful, somewhat lazy, and eager to do something diverting. He, on the other hand, is bound to the Ixion wheel of work. She is at a loss. What can she do? She gets busy herself. Work addiction thus can be "catching," transmitted from husband to wife. I can still remember my wife as my very new bride asking me: "Don't you ever get through working?" It is a question that should be answered with a positive yes.

The Woman Workaholic in the Community

I now ask the same question of my wife as she gets herself involved in one community task after another. (She does not have a paying job.) I saw my mother work in a cotton mill ten hours a day, five and a half days a week, when I was a small child. Therefore—even when I was in professional school and graduate school—it has always been a very important thing to me that our children have their mother in the home. However, in a world in which every third wife is working outside the home, any woman who is not becomes a fair target for all of the institutions, agencies, organizations, fund-raising drives, and volunteer programs that need her services. She, in turn, may get herself overcommitted and become overworked in community activities. She goes about this in certain ways, and for many not-so-obvious reasons.

The value system of a woman tends to shape her workaholism in the community. She may be a religiously devout woman and focus much of her community work in the church. She may be a professionally trained teacher, musician, social worker, or nurse and spend much of her time doing free work that demonstrates her know-how in the field. She may be wealthy and therefore involved in philanthropic work, a member of many agency boards, or the chairman of fund drives. She may be something of a feminist and become absorbed in such efforts as the League of Women Voters or the Women's Liberation Movement. Or she may spend much time at fashion shows, garden clubs, etc. The real dyed-in-the-wool woman workaholic, horror of horrors, is likely to be involved in *all* of these activities. Thus her specific sense of personal identity shapes her community activities and is the drive behind her workaholism.

The woman who becomes addicted to club work, church work, philanthropic work and/or feminist work may well be struggling with her own multitalentedness. Other women may perceive her in this way: "She's *into* everything and she's *good* at everything." She has major trouble, though, in deciding not what she is good at but what she is *best* at and derives the most satisfaction from. In this sense, she has an unresolved identity problem. Rather than let talent and satisfaction guide her, she tries to do *everything*.

Some observations I have made of six workaholic women suggest some hypotheses as to why they are work-addicted. First, five of the six are daughters of men much in the public eye. The five fathers are without exception platform personalities, although their work ranges from medicine and law to the ministry, to business. The daughters are deeply involved with them as public figures. The one woman who is an exception in the group is the daughter of a widowed mother; her father died shortly after she was born. However, the strong masculine people in her life—teachers and pastors—were public figures. My hypothesis is that these women have been role-players modeling themselves after the male figures in their lives. They have a *need for an audience*. What makes them overcommitted work addicts is their drive to be in *every* scene. They cannot watch an action; they have to be in it. (The converse of this tends to be true of sons of public men. They want privacy, ordinarily, and tend to resist group exposure, calls to perform publicly, and the donning of a public image.)

A second hypothesis I have formulated is that the women are in competition with their husbands for public attention. In all six cases, the husband is a quiet, reticent, smiling man who identifies himself primarily as his wife's husband. He *seems* to be happy, although data from other aspects of his life—his health, his concern for the children, and even his concern for his own future—indicate that he is a burdened man. Whenever the husband in these marriages began to gain any public recognition, it was almost routine for the wives to "move in" on his territory. This happens when she, for example, turns his work situation into a social whirl that mobilizes the admiration of the other men and the envy of their wives. I am confident that there is a strong rivalry inherent in the marriage relationship of the community servant type of woman workaholic.

A final characteristic of the community servant type of workaholic is the increased anxiety she experiences when offered a *paid* position. She may take it, but she soon begins to consider herself inadequate. The agreed-upon schedule is usually an impossibly difficult and unrealistic one from the outset. It is not long before she begins to look for a way out of it. This leads to another hypothesis: she wants the responsibility, the position of influence, and the leadership in policy-making, but she does not want the day-to-day responsibility a paid worker has to bear. Yet she shows her impatience and intolerance toward those who do take such a position. This often puts her in conflict with the next kind of woman workaholic—the paid professional woman.

The Work-Addicted Professional Woman

The paid professional woman as a workaholic has many things in common with the men workaholics with whom she works. Whether she be a dyed-in-the-wool, a situational, a pseudo, or an escapist workaholic, she shows many of the same patterns. However, as a woman she differs in many respects.

The Control of Other Women

The largest number of work-addicted women professionals are in paid positions of leadership in so-called women's organizations or in professions predominantly staffed by women. The official women's organizations of religious denominations, for example, are full of them. Besides their own inner compulsions toward work and a ready-made audience of church women, they have idealized religious norms to motivate and sanction their addiction. In the professions, nursing and social work have been largely staffed by women, although some change is taking place at this time, especially in social work. From conversations with a highly competent woman who is both a nurse and a social worker, I formed the hypothesis that the driving force behind the work addiction of women in these professions is the need to control the behavior of other women. This woman operates on the principle that the "early bird gets the worm," arriving at work as much as an hour ahead of everybody else, and getting all her work done first. But she is also the one who insists that everyone leave exactly at quitting time. She disregards the fact that because she arrived early and probably worked through the lunch hour, she had almost two hours of extra time to finish her work. She is extremely critical of peers who keep her late at the office. Yet if a superior of *hers* wants her to stay late, she will do so. Then she makes sure the whole organization knows how indebted the boss is to her for this sacrificial labor. The subtle undertone is that of control.

The Maintenance of an "In" Relationship

Probably one of the main characteristics of the secretary who is a work addict is the sense of power that comes from being on the "inside" of the organizational power structure. She will work at all hours, on Saturdays, Sundays, and holidays. She will forgo vacations for four or five years in succession. She will baby-sit for an executive free of charge. She will travel all night to be the secretary at a secret session of executives. She will help the boss's wife

Christmas-shop, and prepare their personal Christmas cards at night after she gets home. She will accept all sorts of insults, low pay, and a total lack of appreciation. All of this in return for one thing—to know everything that is going to happen before anyone else does, and to know why it happened, straight from the horse's mouth. Her inner supposition, her fantasy, is that such knowledge is power, actual or potential. In brief, the sexual and parental dimensions of the secretary's relationship to her boss have been greatly overemphasized. The power dimensions have been ignored. The desire for power is fuel to work compulsions in women and makes dyed-in-the-wool workaholics of them.

The Correction of Masculine Inadequacy

Another distinctly feminine source of work addiction among professionals is a chronic situational one. The woman may be married to a man who is not fulfilling his husbandly role adequately. The inadequacy may be temporary, as in the case of a husband who is going to school. But the kind of situation deserving most attention here is that in which the woman is married to a chronically inadequate man. Her addiction to work tends to offset this. For example, a very competent social worker marries a patient to whom she was assigned. (The reason he is a patient is that he is slightly retarded and is an alcoholic.) A highly skilled executive secretary is married to a man who has lost each of six jobs in succession. A woman physician is married to a playboy who has an inheritance, spends his time moving from one horse race to another, and sees her only occasionally.

These kinds of women workaholics are a blend of the situational and the escapist type of workaholic. Their station in life vis-à-vis their husbands provides the obvious dynamics for their workaholism. But one inevitably wonders: "Why did they *pick* that kind of husband?" Did their original addiction to work shape their choice of a husband in such a way that their work *could not* be changed by marriage?

Health Hints for Women Workaholics

Some specific suggestions in the form of questions may be helpful for the woman work addict:

First, do you value yourself so little as a woman that you feel you have to exert yourself unreasonably to be accepted, approved, and affirmed? You probably need to explore your own feelings of low self-worth while a colleague in another organization, with a pastoral counselor, with a physician, *and* with a friend whom you can trust.

Second, do all these people whom you *control* through your work pattern really feel loyal to you because of what you do? You might learn from the Taoist proverb: "By not doing, all things are accomplished." If you let up, and get to work when your coworkers do—even *after* they do occasionally—and demand your vacation and accumulated sick leave, you will very likely create affection around you by exercising these rights. Your family and friends and co-workers will feel, "She is finally becoming human," and will want your company more often.

Finally, don't you want to do some of the things women do for fun? Go out with some friends to a nice place for lunch, even daring to come back a half hour late. Visit a hairdresser and the women's health club in your town. Take some money and splurge at a fancy salon where they offer facials, manicures, massages, steam baths. Go window-shopping at lunch time another day. Find a safe place to sit that has a beautiful view and sit and do nothing! You can learn something from your own pregnancy or that of others at this "just sitting." When the pregnant woman is sitting still, doing nothing, she is accomplishing everything. The mystery of the physiology of a woman is a symbol of the creativity of the capacity to cooperate with rather than to try to force nature. The silent wisdom of the body teaches the relationship between work and rest, growth and repose, effort and release. A rhythm of being is inherent that in the sophistication of our civilization and artificiality we have either not learned consciously or have forgotten. It can be learned; it can be remembered; it can be taught. The symbolism of the "work" of the birth process is a silent antithesis to the frenetic activity of the workaholic. For that reason this symbolism is the parable that both male and female workaholics have to learn in order to be genuinely productive and at peace with oneself at one and the same time.

VIII
The Religion
of the Workaholic

A certain kind of *devotion* seeps through every aspect of a *confirmed* workaholic's being. He is over*committed* to his work.

As you reread the above paragraph, you see the italicized words *devotion, confirmed,* and *committed.* Placed in an ecclesiastical context, these words can become "god talk." Work is a kind of religion to the workaholic. The plan here is to describe the religious situation of the confirmed or dyed-in-the-wool work-aholic, to reflect upon the meaning of conversion as a psychological process in the life of the workaholic, and to discuss the positive faith of a person who is a converted workaholic.

The Future of the Workaholic

The workaholic is a person who has trouble with the future. He elides the future with the present to such an extent that he destroys the present in the process. This means to me that he pins his hopes on what he can do to ward off the specters of meaninglessness, poverty, calamity, and hopelessness that the very idea of the future represents to him. Yet the crucial factor in a healthy religion is hope—a belief in the unseen realities of the present and the future. Lack of such belief, and the associated feeling that everything must happen immediately or not at all, is the real religious problem of the workaholic. The concern of the person guiding the religious life of the workaholic, then, should be to come to grips with his pervasive feeling of futurelessness.

The Religious Situation of the Confirmed Workaholic

A Child of His Times

The confirmed workaholic is a man of unclean lips in his worship of work, to paraphrase the prophet Isaiah, and he lives amongst people who are also of unclean lips. Yet he practices a highly sanctioned way of life. Some people have identified it as a Protestant malady, but close observation of Catholics and Jews indicates that they suffer from the addiction as much as do Protestants. The so-called Protestant work ethic can be summarized as follows: a universal taboo is placed on *idleness,* and *industriousness* is considered a religious ideal; *waste* is a vice, and *frugality* a virtue; complacency and failure are outlawed, and *ambition* and *success* are taken as sure signs of God's favor; the universal sign of sin is *poverty,* and the crowning sign of God's favor is *wealth.* The Hebrew Bible is filled with evidence of this way of life; the prudential ethic of the Book of Proverbs is one reflection of it, and the kinds of questions the disciples asked of Jesus, are another—for example, when the rich young man turned away from Jesus, the disciples asked: "Who then can be saved?" My point is that the workaholic's personal religion—quite apart from his denominational affiliation—reflects the ethic of industriousness, frugality, ambition, and success as primary virtues. To reject these is to go against the grain of his religious culture. Honoring them, he has the sanction of his religious community, which not only approves his ideals but gladly welcomes his financial contributions. That he may be idolatrous in respect to his own achievements does not even come into question.

A Victim of Success

In earlier times, success and wealth as assurances of salvation most often came at the end of a man's life span. Not many men long survived the period of reaching the top. Now, however, the life span of Americans has increased to such an extent that when workaholics achieve worldly success they generally still have ten to thirty years of life ahead of them. Where do they go from the "top"?

Success has a way of becoming a burden in a society in which there are so many pseudo workaholics who take ambition and success seriously without taking industry and frugality to heart at all. Their only hope is to "fake it," modeling their behavior on that of the so-called heroes of the work faith, the true work addicts. But sometimes success may become such a burden to work addicts that they want out. They may misbehave in some way—revert to an old pattern of wine or women (but this time no song); put their hand into the company till; or get into difficulties with the establishment and get fired.

A few more fortunate people will be like the five men described in a recent issue of *Life* magazine. All these men had achieved success—one as a salesman, one as a stockbroker, one an insurance executive, one a veterinarian, and one a policeman. They all changed their type of work to something that let them *live* as well as work. They were between the ages of thirty-five and fifty—as *Life* says, "the years of heightened susceptibility to alcohol, heart attack, worry, and divorce." They all had the enthusiastic cooperation of their wives; as one of them said, "I knew she was the kind who wasn't a prestige seeker, or I wouldn't have married her in the first place." [1]

These persons have gotten off the success treadmill. They may work as much as ever, but with a difference: they are not compelled to do so, they share their work with their families, and they are doing what they enjoy. They have renewed their lives.

Not many people make such leaps. To do so is so newsworthy that it is written up in a popular national magazine. The great majority who become victims of

[1] *Life,* June 12, 1970, p. 56.

success stay in a field or job long after it has lost its challenge. Too often they wait for sickness or accident to make the decision for them. Many die without getting a second wind in life. The greatest tragedy is that the springs of both joy and creativity dry up in their lives. Many suffer until the age of retirement. They are obviously successful but on the defensive with the whole world. This may even be worse than death.

Characteristics of the Personal Religion of the Work Addict

When we dare enter the private sanctuary of the confirmed work addict's personal religion, we find an ambiguous interplay of contrasting values. It is not pure light or pure darkness. For example, the work addict is a blend of loneliness and solitude. Loneliness is the hopeless side of being by oneself; solitude is the joyful side. He may be a sporadic church attender. He may have the desire instead to go back to his work if he can be there alone, unbothered by the other employees; this is a rather common and unnoticed ritual of many people. Or, he may have worked himself, as Viktor Frankl says, into stupefaction and want simply to be alone. He may be so preoccupied that he does not want to be with his family. Thus his loneliness appears.

But on the other hand, being by himself may instead produce some of his most creative times of communion with God, with nature, with himself, and all the regenerative forces of his life. His survival as a person may depend on his being alone. This is a paradox. He may choose not to go to church because he will just encounter more people and more voices there. Unlike the farmer who may have worked in comparative solitude all week, he has been in meetings, heard and delivered speeches and exhortations, dealt with public and community problems all week. To go to church is a "rerun." He prefers a religion of solitude as one way of maintaining the integrity of his being. As Nicholas Berdyaev says: "Only when man is alone . . . does he become aware of his personality, of his originality, of his singularity and uniqueness, of his distinctness from every one and every thing else. A man may feel himself definitely more alone in the midst of his co-religionists than in the midst of men of totally different beliefs and persuasions." [2] Lord Byron expressed something of the inner world of each of us when he wrote in *Childe Harold's Pilgrimage:*

> There is a pleasure in the pathless woods,
> There is a rapture on the lonely shore,
> There is society where none intrudes,
> By the deep sea, and music in its roar;
> I love not Man the less but Nature more,
> From these our interviews, in which I steal
> From all I may be, or have been before,
> To mingle with the Universe, and feel
> What I can ne'er express, yet cannot all conceal.

Narrowed Consciousness and Meditation

Times of solitude in the workaholic's life widen his consciousness and put him in touch with what is really important in life. But they are rare indeed, for his ordinary way of life is highly constricted. His area of consciousness is greatly narrowed. He is aware of this and has several phrases for it: he says he is in a rut; he is chained to the

[2] *Solitude and Society* (London: The Centenary Press, 1938), pp. 68-69, 92.

oars like a galley slave; he labors in the salt mines; he has his nose to the grindstone. However he describes it, he becomes anxious at the thought of what he is missing, at how short life is, and at what a hurry he is in.

In theological language, this narrowed perspective of the job as the sum total of existence is what Paul Tillich called idolatry. Something less than God is treated and valued *as if* it were God; a *limited* concern is put in the place of the unlimited and ultimate concern in life. The end result is to turn one's life over to the demonic, to become possessed—in this case by one's job.

The work addict may be said to have a *poverty* of objects of attention. He is bound to the automatic perceptions, feelings, and centers of awareness of his job. He cannot see the whole architecture of life because he has his eye on one brick. Nor can he *feel* anything except that it is *he* who holds that brick in place, and that if he did not the whole structure would collapse. Furthermore, he acts as if that whole structure upholds the universe. None of this is so.

Persons involved in religious institutions seem to be particularly vulnerable to this kind of idolatry. It is one thing for a minister or religious worker to sing: "I love Thy Church, O Lord; her walls before me stand. . . ." It is quite another to fix one's eye upon those walls so closely that he cannot see the Lord or anything else! Such a person needs a diversionary kind of work, preferably a skilled trade that he enjoys in order to establish his separation from the church as an idol. I know a minister who is a skilled cabinet-maker. He has made beautiful furniture for his own home and sold a few pieces for fun. He *could* make his living at it. This both liberates him and reminds his church people that they do not own him. Doing this work in his leisure time, he finds that his whole perspective on his other responsibilities is widened.

Religion of Works and Productivity

Another characteristic of the religion of the confirmed workaholic is that he seeks to *merit* everything he gets. The idea of unearned acceptance and love, commonly called "grace" in theological language, is known to him only intellectually if at all.

Much has been said by theologians in the vein of Dietrich Bonhoeffer about "cheap grace," that is, a religion that salves people's consciences and lulls them into moral inattention to great social issues. Bonhoeffer had seen this during the Hitler regime. We see evidences of it in America today. Such psychotherapists as O. Hobart Mowrer argue that we have pushed the business of redemption without proper amends in good works too far. Yet the workaholic is a compulsive caricature of Bonhoeffer's and Mowrer's best intention. He does not take forgiveness from God or anyone else without paying, and paying, and paying. He is a person who *works* his way into your heart. He produces everything—on his own.

Childish Omnipotence

The reason the workaholic has a religion of work and works is that he or she thus maintains the illusion of all-powerfulness. He tries to be his own god, a trait which Sigmund Freud said is characteristic of the human race. The illusion tends to erase awareness of personal death and leaves us with the assumption that we are not only all-powerful but immortal.

Fatalism and Harsh Realism

A final characteristic of the confirmed work addict's religion is that he is a fatalist. He will, upon reading this book, say: "Yes. Much of what you say is true, but there is nothing anybody can do about it. It has always been this way and always will be." This means that he deeply feels that he has no power of decision over his own life. He is realistic to a fault. He always expects the worst and has never been disappointed; if things by chance do turn out well, it is the result of accident, luck, or winning against impossible odds. This is the sort of opinion which of course cannot be disconfirmed. Little wonder he relies upon magic—his own.

The Workaholic at Church

No discussion of the workaholic's religion is complete without an appraisal of him as a churchman. For many workaholics, the job is their church, and the actual church is a place for their wives and children, to which they themselves go only under social pressure. Once the workaholic gets there, he is preoccupied with events of the last week and plans for the next. Physically, he is present; spiritually, he is not. I recall one morning when a woman and her husband sat next to us at church. She had to punch her husband in the ribs to get him to put their offering in the plate as it passed. We all chuckled quietly together. He said: "She had to tell me to write the check before we left home. Now she has to tell me to put it in the plate." She remarked: "He was a long way from here." I said: "Your husband and I really would be at a loss without our wives when we are at church!"

On the other hand, there are some workaholics who make of church itself another form of their addiction. They arise early and go to bed late each Sunday. Every available moment in between is filled with an assignment of church work. The religion is another form of the compulsion.

When I was a pastor of a small church in the Bluegrass section of Kentucky, a mother of a fourteen-year-old boy brought him to me after the evening service. She said to me: "What am I going to do with Gordon? He would not come to church this afternoon. He wanted to play. He got mad. He said, 'Church, church, church! That's all I hear!' Now, Mr. Oates, what do you think of him?" The boy was terribly embarrassed. I said to him: "Gordon, I know exactly how you feel. All *I* hear is 'church,' and sometimes I get tired. And when I get real tired of church the next time, I am coming to see you, because I know you will understand." Then I turned to his mother and said: "Anybody who has never gotten tired of church just never has been to church much."

At its positive core, though, the religion of the workaholic may not be even a Sunday religion. It is an overworked weekday religion of practical good deeds to other people. He knocks himself out helping people, but unless he is converted he does so as a means of controlling them, placing them in his debt, or at least making them feel uneasy. It is not until a basic change takes place in him that this doing good becomes less ambiguous and more relaxed, a source of pleasure.

The Process of Conversion in the Life of a Work Addict

The radical self-encounter that resulted in my own right-about-face in my work habits has been referred to from time to time in this book. When I draw it all together, I would summarize it this way. The first dawnings of awareness came to me through my sons who insisted as little boys that I change my ways. I took them seriously, but only partly mended my ways. The second phase of self-confrontation came in a period when I was suffering from a pinched signal nerve. Whenever I overworked, it would throw me down, at times literally. The real spiritual crisis came when my sons were old enough to have a minimum need of me and when, due to successful surgery on the third attempt, my back was made strong and well. Then I had to face the fact that I had made a fetish and idol of work, that institutional commitments were really overcommitments, that life was really meant to be enjoyed without paying for it with work, that I needed people for their own sakes and not as a means of accomplishing my work goals, and that the *now* of life is the nectar of being.

Probably what drove me to the bottom of the pit of despair was my agony over the safety of our elder son. He was a combat sailor, a machine-gunner on a small river assault boat in the Mekong Delta in Vietnam for a year. I was helpless. None of *my* actions or work could change a thing. I found myself falling back heavily on extra work to handle my anxiety. When for two months I had no work responsibility in the summer, my major defense was gone. I faced it alone before God. I realized that I could not face it alone, but that I needed God's help and the help of all the other people I could get. I learned to laugh at my work compulsions and, as Viktor Frankl terms it, to "de-reflect" them. I shifted my attention to the things I fundamentally enjoyed thinking about and doing, and I did these things. For example, when it came to accepting an extra engagement for more work, I used a new criterion— not *should* I do this, or *must* I do this?—but will this be enjoyable, will it be fun, in the sense of the Westminster Catechism: "The chief end of man is to glorify God and to enjoy him forever." The criterion I am using now is thus not enjoying myself in the superficial sense, but enjoyment of God wherever *he is,* not was, not will be. Sam Keen put what was happening to me best: "I was coming home to the obvious. After squandering much of my time in the future and the past I was returning to my native time—the present. I had not learned how to cultivate the now, to live gracefully in the present, to love the actual, but I was no longer in exile." [3]

This is the simple unraveling of preoccupation, because being "somewhere else" is either *yesterday* or *tomorrow,* not *now*. Living in the moment means the release of much of that irritability which we feel toward someone here-and-now who tries to pull us out of the past or future into the present. Furthermore, it reduces our haste, because if we *are* where we intend to be, why hurry to get some place else? And it does away with much depression, because frequently sadness arises from reliving the past or from apprehensiveness for the future.

This is all dramatically illustrated by an experience I had in the airport at Birmingham, Alabama. I had gotten to the airport late and was running wildly past other people in the concourse to get to my flight. I passed two men, who said: "Hey, mister, don't hurry." I stopped suddenly, turned about, and said: "Why?" One of them answered: "Because *we* are the pilots of your flight!" We all broke into laughter. So—if the pilot is in no hurry, why should I be?

The Psychology of the Workaholic's Conversion

Some of the ideas of Harry M. Tiebout about the psychological effects of conversion upon addiction patterns in alcoholics are useful in widening our perspective on the process in workaholics.

Tiebout describes the alcoholic as tense, depressed, aggressive or at least quietly stubborn, oppressed with feelings of inferiority and at the same time acting quite superior, perfectionistic, and rigid, overpowered with a sense of loneliness, basically self-centered, defiant, living

[3] *The Dance of Life* (New York: Harper & Row, 1970), p. 21.

in a world apart from others. I have said that work as well as alcohol aids and abets these tendencies and when pursued compulsively will produce a similar personality profile. The process of conversion comes from the group experience of challenge by a more positive set of attitudes. Essentially both alcohol and work addictions are negations of life. The group conversion process challenges this negation by making possible a personal affirmation of life. It is a definite choice of life as opposed to death. Tiebout says that religion "Too often has been identified with its dogmas and not its essence of spirituality. It is not the form religion takes; it is its function in achieving a frame of mind that is significant." [4] I would modify his statement somewhat to say that dogma is too often a screen for the things that make workaholics of men: prestige, accumulation of material goods, and the exercise of self-effort, as opposed to the satisfactions of belonging to an accepting fellowship.

The Religious Outlook of the Converted Workaholic

I have already given a general description of the lifestyle of the converted workaholic. Here I want to discuss his specific religious situation. He is not completely different, but neither will he ever be the same again.

A Forgiving Attitude

The genuinely converted workaholic is aware that his own estimate of competence is in itself incomplete. If he perceived himself as a "prophet of competence" prior to his conversion, now he knows that his prophecies are incomplete. He still values his competence highly. Yet he

[4] "Conversion as a Psychological Phenomenon (in the Treatment of the Alcoholic)," *Pastoral Psychology*, April, 1951, p. 34.

allows *lebensraum* or spiritual territory for those around him and even actively searches for specific examples of their unique abilities. These are the topics of his conversation instead of the person's weaknesses, incompetency, and unworthiness. He becomes patient instead of intolerant.

A Sense of Irony and Humor

As the workaholic develops a new way of life, he learns how to stand off from himself and his fellow workers from time to time and laugh ironically *at* himself and humorously *with* them as they laugh at themselves. Because the converted workaholic now has a more secure, self-accepting attitude toward himself, he can jestingly say to others some fairly hard negative things about himself which they themselves half believe but do not have the courage to say. And their perception of his inner strength allows them to laugh with him. For example, any person who works as much with the mentally ill as I do is likely to be thought of by a few people as somewhat odd in his own right. I simply admit it! People enjoy it when I say it. In my previous way of life, I could not have said it humorously, and if someone else had, it would have been a high insult.

A more important observation is that this irony and humor spring from a person's new awareness that God's acceptance is freely given and not earned by the sweat of one's brow.

A Sense of Wonder and Awe

The harassed workaholic has little time or appreciation for the experience of wonder and awe. For example, it is now over a year ago that our son returned from the war. I am always filled with awe and wonder when I see him—strong, safe, well, and happy. He brought back with him a quiet devotion to the children of Vietnam. I can participate in the beauty and tragedy of these children's lives, and I am able to participate in the lives of all children. The world of nature—plants, flowers, and animals has widened the range of my attention. I have become keenly aware again that reading is for exploration and adventure and not just for the sake of title-dropping or keeping up with the academic Joneses. At the same time, I do not read as much as before because I now am able to experience wonder and awe in conversation with people, and from a few television shows and some movies and stage plays.

A De-Programming of Corporate Worship

Much effort goes into the programming of the religious behavior of people. Some of this effort is expended by unreconstructed, religion-oriented workaholics. The religion of the converted workaholic certainly is not one of disdain for the results of these people's labors and most certainly not for the people themselves. However, the converted workaholic hopes that the religionists will come face-to-face with themselves before old age and retirement force them into a corner of unmitigated disgust, despair, and hopelessness.

The hopes of the *un*converted workaholic are almost always *deferred* hopes, religiously speaking. He thinks as Kipling did in his "L'Envoi":

> When Earth's last picture is painted, and the tubes
>   are twisted and dried,
> When the oldest colours have faded, and the youngest
>   critic has died,
> We shall rest, and, faith, we shall need it—
>   lie down for an aeon or two,
> Till the Master of all good workmen
>   shall put us to work anew. . . .

And only the Master shall praise us, and only the
    Master shall blame;
And no one shall work for money, and no one
    shall work for fame,
But each for the joy of working, and each, in his
    separate star,
Shall draw the Thing as he sees It for the God of
    Things as they are!

This kind of *deferred* gratification in the hereafter is a
positive consolation for the scourge that work is here-
and-now. What I wish for, however, is the de-programming
of such deferred hopes. *Some* of these aspirations should
be realized in the present. If churches will settle for less
real estate, less "money and fame," and fewer structures of
organized religion, the enjoyment of God will more be
more possible to more people more often.

The converted workaholic tends normally to keep his
need for solitude. Going to church can nourish this need
in a very positive way, for one can experience a degree of
solitude and at the same time be accessible to other church
members. Some people I know live and breathe as a
somewhat inconspicuous part of their church. They do not
try to become acquainted with everyone in the congrega-
tion. They know a few people in profound intimacy, but
do not take the activist approach to church life and worship. Some specific types of people in the church—for
example, the older people, the little children, and occasionally an adolescent who has trouble belonging to the
teen-age "scene"—have a deep appreciation for the person
who lives his life in slower motion. The converted work
addict can find a quiet fellowship with these persons.
Then, too, there are always a few other people whose
experience with work has been similar to his. They too
can provide comradeship.

The Catholic Church reveres Joseph, the father of

Jesus, as a saint. They sing a hymn to him, one stanza of which is as follows:

> Joseph, workmen's inspiration, man of faith and charity
> Make us honest, faithful, strong
> With Christ true liberty,
> Make our labor and our leisure
> Fruitful to eternity.

The idea of labor and leisure both being fruitful to eternal life is the highest good of the converted workaholic's faith.

The mix of work and leisure in faith is best nurtured in our accepting the fellowship of people who share our problems, can make a common confession of their plight, and join in a quest for a more sane way of living. One of the prayers that I have in writing this book is that it will become a basis of communication out of which will grow groups of persons who share the dilemmas of work addiction. Being a churchman of sorts myself, I hope that churches may be one of the meeting grounds for these purposes. But I hope that they will not be the only ones. I could hope that management concerns, business establishments, schools, and universities will be places of meeting also. All of these, like the church, tend to be ghettoes of a sort. I hope this book will open new ways of life and help men and women break out of old ones.

IX
The Remaking of the Life
of the Workaholic

The essence of hope rests in the conviction that life is worth living and that a person's life can be made better, can actually be remade. These are the alternatives to futility. The workaholic has lived his or her life on a long treadmill. His life must be remade in order for him even to dare hope it can become an eventful pilgrimage toward new events and satisfactions. As it takes that course he will discover that challenging climbs of effort are followed by vast vistas of new insight and pleasant valleys of satisfaction: a journey different from the dead level one on the treadmill known better as despair. This radical change *can* happen but it does not *just* happen. The purpose of this concluding chapter is to locate and describe some of the powerful factors which induce these changes and some of the habits that maintain the changes as a way of life instead of a passing enthusiasm.

The Jarring Realizations of Suffering

Suffering is really a messenger to the workaholic. The basic issue is: can the work addict hear the message over the clatter of his compulsions? I once was called as a chaplain to the bedside of a minister. His doctor had told him to put his personal and family life in order because he had only a few days to live. I had known this man earlier. He had all the characteristics of work addiction. He spoke of himself as a fighter at all times of crisis. Here was a crisis that fighting only aggravated and did not solve or alleviate. He "surrendered" when he was told that death was at hand. As he did so, he relaxed and became more serene. His whole body was less tense. Days in the hospital went by, and he did not die. Weeks went by, and he began to improve. He was finally discharged from the hospital with a strict prescription of limited duty. He stayed by his strict routine—and lived eight and one half years longer. It was as if he had been given a reprieve in return for giving up his compulsive work habits.

This kind of encounter with suffering has a way of delivering a person from the treadmill of activity. It teaches him how to value each moment for its own sake rather than as a meaningless interspace between fits of work. Fyodor Dostoevsky demonstrates this in his thoughts before receiving a reprieve from a firing squad. "What an eternity! What if I did not have to die. All eternity would be mine. Oh, then I would change every minute into a century; I would not lose a single one; I would keep track of all my instincts, and I would not spend any of them lightly." The business of living in the past or the future to the light disregard of the happiness of the present would have to go if we have once faced the abyss of death.

But my point is that one need not have such loud messages as impending death by a heart attack or facing a firing squad to hear what suffering has to say about the faulty way of life of work addiction. We can even learn common sense from the common cold. In a day when antibiotics are supposed to do everything for us, we expect them to instantly cure the cold and fever that throws us. Yet colds are, in effect, one way nature has of reminding us that we have not taken a day off for weeks. Our unenjoyed weekends are catching up with us.

The voice of illness is persistent and should be heard. When it does come, the person wrongly related to work will find himself making decisions he should have had the good judgment to make earlier: he leaves certain tasks undone, he gets someone else to—or *lets* someone else—do others, and he finds that a few were of no consequence to anyone anyhow! As Richard Cabot, the distinguished physician at Massachusetts General Hospital, used to say:

"The body has more sense than the mind." It was he who coined the phrase "the wisdom of the body" that was used by Alexis Carrell later for a book by that title.[1]

Suffering, however, may not come to some persons in the form of physical pain. Rather, they find themselves hopelessly and permanently involved in one interpersonal conflict after another. Their lives are a constant uproar. These people get so involved in fighting battles that they lose the war. Their preoccupation with themselves keeps them from paying attention to specific transactions going on between them and people for whom and to whom they are responsible. This sort of suffering seems to be characteristic of persons in various kinds of administrative positions. It seems to be an occupational hazard of administrators that they are tone-deaf to the feelings people express to them, unless and until they are violently expressed. They tend not to hear quiet, rational expressions of negative feelings, reasonable criticisms, and even-tempered suggestions for change. In this era of confrontation, being tone-deaf is asking for trouble. Administrators themselves, therefore, come upon evil days of trouble in their own right, ranging from resignations of professionals, to strikes of non-professional and skilled workers, to mass protests, to violence.

I am not condoning anti-establishment behavior for its own sake, of course. I am simply pointing to the fact that it can perhaps be understood partly in terms of the administrators themselves. *Why* are they not more in tune with the people they are dealing with? I would suggest three things. First, administrators have and take little or no time for meditation. Meditation means getting in touch with oneself. As Clark Moustakas says, "Being alone with one's self enables the person to reflect on his experience,

[1] *The Wisdom of the Body* (New York: Halcyon, 1935).

to perceive and examine the parameters of a real issue or problem, and to engage openly and freely in thought and feeling. At the same time, there is a letting go, so that images and thoughts move in and out until a single dimension emerges, which becomes the center of intensive exploration. Through meditation, new facets of the self enter awareness, and opportunities for growth and development are revealed." [2] To be without this is to have one's consciousness progressively constricted.

A second factor in the situation of the administrator is that he is usually imprisoned in his job. Where else from the so-called top can you go? About three years ago, a group of university presidents were surveyed by a national magazine. Several of them said that such positions should be for specific terms of five to ten years. Then a man should be expected by society to go into other types of work. I heartily agree and have seen a few men who acted on the principle. In these few instances their influence increased as their involvement in officialdom decreased. In other words, administrative responsibility should be an *era* of life and not a way of life. If an administrator can see the sense of this, he is probably not a workaholic. If he cannot, he probably is.

The third feature of the administrator's way of life is that he is addicted to the role and despises the function he has in life. He revels in the perquisites, place, and public exposure of his job, but he despises the tasks associated with it—raising money, maintaining good personal relationships, and negotiating clear, well-defined and secure contacts with individuals and groups. This ambivalence ties him to his own brand of repetitive, meaningless tasks.

[2] *Personal Growth: The Struggle for Identity and Human Values* (Cambridge, Mass.: Howard A. Doyle Publishing Company, 1969), p. 21.

However, he *can* break out of the situation if he has a minimum of face to lose, and if he wants to do so. Yet, if he is afraid of losing face because he cuts down on the number of programs he initiates, admits that other plans are unrealistic, and others are unwise, he will continue to be committed to a futile scheme of things. Wholesome discovery *could* take place in the line organization of a company, a school, a hospital, a church, a denomination, a nation if the leaders and those who work for them could meet on a common ground—their addiction to the constricted confines of their particular work. The average organization is painfully in need of such ventilation, clarification, and redirection.

Such a group meeting could effectively begin with *admonition*. In this phase each member would advise the others on how to change their work habits. This would allow the perfectionism and intolerance of each person to get out in the open. One person might say to another: "You can turn out more work than I can, but I get the feeling that the *reason* you do so is to make all the rest of us as uncomfortable as we can be."

A second group meeting should continue with *confession*. Here each person is not allowed to rebut the admonitions he or she has received, nor to add to the suggestions he has made to others. He is allowed only to say what is wrong with his own work pattern. Thus, his own feelings of inferiority, despair, and hopelessness are expressed. In the presence of his own working colleagues, he is enabled to separate his own work accomplishments and industry from his deeply buried feelings of inferiority. For example, one person in such a group I attended said that she had produced a great many star pupils through her teaching. She loved to call people's attention to what these students were doing. But, she confessed, she had begun to realize there was a connection between this and the fact that she and her husband could not have children. Much of her creation of star pupils was a substitute for not having children of her own. Moreover, she was beginning to see that she treated these students as children, not adults, for the same reason.

In the third group session, each member should be encouraged to challenge the self-estimates of the other members of the group. Not yet do they answer each other's criticism vented in the "admonition" session. Rather each is required to affirm, encourage, and sustain others against the weight of self-reproach. For example, one man might say to another, "You think you are no good at making speeches, but when I say something I feel like you are the only one who really hears what I mean."

In another session, the members of the group may be asked to respond to earlier comments about themselves, to express feelings of being misunderstood by the group and reasons why they therefore feel alone in this company of people. This may bring to the surface the old feelings that make workaholics of them. For example, one man said he had always felt that he had to "try harder" because he did not come from the well-to-do social class that other group members did. He felt they misunderstood him because they saw him as a very urbane, polished person of great culture. One member in the first session, for example, had said: "You have the edge on us because you were born with a silver spoon in your mouth and we were not." He really was not. Now this man's "proud inferiority" could be told. He said: "I actually was born on the wrong side of the tracks and had a real alley-cat education."

Additional group meetings can be held without a fixed agenda. If an administrator has the time and the courage to initiate such group meditation, he himself may discover a new way of life. He may find a way other than pay, promotion, penalty, and reward to communicate with his staff, at a genuinely human level. If he feels that his position prevents this, then he can provide a skilled group leader to catalyze this kind of sharing of the sufferings of workingmen.

My hypothesis here is that the sufferings of the work addict are both physical and interpersonal. The effective leader in an organization recognizes this. Instead of scourging his people "like quarry slaves to their dungeons" at night and on the weekends, a leader who is willing to make himself a part of the process helps to affirm and renew his colleagues by a group-process approach to their work addiction.[3]

Anguish: Withdrawal Symptoms

Once a workaholic admits that he is "hooked" on work, he faces a time of anguish and agony as he begins the process of disengagement from work addiction. For all practical purposes, he suffers from withdrawal symptoms. These are some of the hallmarks of withdrawal:

1. *Telephonitis:* For years this person has done much of his work by making telephone calls at night and/or on the weekend. Now he suffers the pangs of acute anxiety as he leaves those calls for the next morning or for the beginning of the next week. This takes major habit-reconditioning, family support, and constant perseverance.

2. *Untangling Overattachment to the Plant or the Office.* The busy salesman has a way of leaving his paper work until the evening or weekend. The plant foreman brings

---

[3] For additional suggestions, see: Michael S. Olmsted, *The Small Group* (New York: Random House, 1959), and John Hendrix, *On Becoming a Group* (Nashville: Broadman Press, 1969).

home the payroll data to compile in the evenings. The professor brings papers home to grade or leaves his next day's preparation until the evening. Breaking this habit brings all the anxiety of a withdrawal syndrome. A metal company executive told me in a leisurely evening conversation in his home that he steadfastly resolved to leave the job at the office. He said that he had decided to quit overwork "cold turkey," all at once, and described having stood outside his office building for a half hour on a winter night struggling against returning to get unfinished work to take home. He finally altered his work habits after much struggle of this kind.

3. *Disciplining the Need to Lengthen the Day.* This same man had to make a compromise with his initial resolve. He decided that instead of taking work home, he would stay on the job until he finished it. The first week he had to stay at the office until nine o'clock. The second day he was able to leave at 7:30. It took him two months to achieve his goal: to have dinner at 6:30 each evening with his family. Once he got the habit established and was enjoying his family's praise for doing so, he was able to maintain it.

4. *Ego-Deprivation.* Another set of withdrawal symptoms centers around the feeling of being a "has-been." The workaholic remembers the time he was in the middle of everything. He is likely to be lured into a regression or relapse into workaholism by feelings of ego-deprivation at not being on every committee, in every available leadership position, continuously in the spotlight. The cryptic wisdom of Thomas à Kempis is a hard saying for the workaholic: "No man safely appears abroad until he has learned how quietly to stay at home out of sight." This does not mean that the workaholic becomes a hermit. No. He needs people deeply. Rather it means that he

learns a new meaning of influence, namely the power of invisible influence, that which is effected as a kind of secret service. One hand does not know what the other does. Alms are not given to be seen by men.

Positive Reinforcement

Yesterday my wife said to our daughter-in-law: ". . . that was back when my husband had to spend so much time on the phone." I caught the phrase and said to her later, "What do you think has caused phone calls to take less of my time at home now?" We agreed it was because I had given up some of my extra jobs and had quit doing my work at home. She reinforced the decisions I had made with positive appreciation.

This is where the family of the converted workaholic can help. As has been indicated, some—not all—of the factors in work addiction are family expectations. If these can be changed and positive appreciation given for *not* overworking, then a happy work pattern can be more easily established.

Another source of positive reinforcement comes from one's intimate co-workers. In the work unit of which I am a part, we find real help for each other in the joint discussion of new duties any one of us is about to assume. We affirm each other's decisions to live sensibly as to amounts and kinds of work and sources of motivation and satisfaction as we do the work. We admonish each other when we see ourselves being unwise or even foolish about work. Each of us has a caring community to help us correct our tendency to act all-powerful and be everywhere. An atmosphere of humor and banter pervades these conversations. I cannot adequately describe the deep appreciation I feel for the ways in which these co-workers, to whom this book is dedicated, have seriously kidded me into a more creative and wholesome attitude toward work. Many of the ideas in these pages are understandings we have learned to act on together.

One of the sources of work addiction is the need for approval and admiration of those whose judgment we value. Therefore, it is important that the ethos of an organization be slanted toward wisdom and temperance. Recently I sat in the office of an executive who said: "I can remember when there was such a good morale in our company that you could come here any night and find men burning the midnight oil in their work. But this is no longer the case. I hope we can get back to that spirit." Here the expectations were actually built around a work-addiction ethic.

I recall a meeting of a mental health society in which the speaker was an outstanding psychiatrist. In his remarks he emphasized the importance of play as well as work, laughter as well as seriousness. He prescribed a "golden mean" between these opposites. After he had finished, an award was given to the outstanding mental health worker in the state hospital system. The award was given to a man who had served the system remarkably well. But in the actual wording of the citation he was complimented for not having had a vacation for several years! The ambiguity about what mental health *is* could not have been dramatized more ironically. The approval constituted by the award was a reinforcement of work addiction.

A contrary pattern is found in one theological seminary which is closed completely for one whole month each year. In order to keep anyone from refusing this period of rest, they turn off the electricity and water and change the locks so people's keys will not let them in to work. This is an organization that means it when they say "vacation time." They use an "approval system" that conditions men and women toward a healthy work pattern. The end results are a qualitatively *better* kind of work during the rest of the year. People do not work beyond the point of effectiveness in their tasks. Such a modification of the approval system offsets the withdrawal syndrome, whereas others I have described exaggerate it.

Grace: The Antidote of Workaholism

The kind of atmosphere created by an approval system in an organization that reinforces wise and healthy work patterns is generated by an attitude of grace and not law. The theological concept of "grace" means that God's attitude toward a wrongdoer is one of free, spontaneous, and unconditional favor and love. Grace is offered to a man because it accomplishes good things for him that he cannot do for himself. A person can approve himself, but he needs another who validates that approval.

Furthermore, grace has the element of gratitude and appreciation in it. The *grace* of God rests upon a person in his work. Likewise, grace covers imperfection and fault; one does not always have to be perfect. It is not a man's work that merits a place in God's favor, but the fact that he is a person created in the image of God, kin to God.

The converted workaholic, therefore, is a person who takes this grace in life on faith. He begins with an affirmation of himself that precedes all organic handicaps of body and health, that precedes all the "devil's messages" he may have received from parents and siblings as to what he can and cannot do, that precedes the somewhat artificial estimates of potential success or failure he may have experienced in the school system. That self-affirmation rests on the fact that he is created in the image of God and is therefore received, accepted, and loved by God. Whether a person is Jew, Catholic, or Protestant, he can begin here. From this basepoint of existence, he can begin to use his faith in grace to offset his constant need to prove that he is acceptable by more and more work. This is in fact the antidote for work addiction.

However, the world around the work addict must put some flesh and blood around the abstract concept of grace. The community of labor that treats its workers as if they were property of the management cannot communicate this grace. Grace is an event that occurs between persons and persons, not persons and things. A community of labor that treats its workers as mentally inferior and therefore open to manipulation by people who perceive themselves as astute, clever, and extremely knowledgeable cannot communicate grace. Grace is an experience that takes place between persons who perceive each other as responsible and trustworthy, not inferior.

The community of labor that embodies grace in relation to its workers expresses that grace as follows:

1. The community of labor establishes clear and well-defined covenants of employment and keeps its promises, to those who work. If it is impossible to keep these promises, the exact reasons are explained and a new covenant formed. If there is doubt as to who is right, the person in the position of disadvantage is given the benefit of the doubt. As my mentor, Olin Binkley, is fond of saying, "Everybody wins in a contest of kindness."

2. The community of labor embodying grace has the typical merit system of reward built into the promotion and pay increase system, but it also makes sure to celebrate the achievements of its workers. For example, some organizations celebrate the fifth, tenth, twentieth anni-

versaries of their employees' service. Some faculties, administrations, or departments celebrate when a member of the faculty has a book published. The community of work that does not generate a steady pattern of appreciation of its members tends to go to seed in a system of coercion and demand, not praise and encouragement.

In the organization without grace, a reward is given for "behaving" and a penalty is exacted for nonconformity. One of the most common causes of workaholism is such institutional deprivation. The workplace is a labor camp, not a labor community. The leadership that has to be told this is already disqualified. The essence of grace is that it is unprompted.

The church of a work addict is the official custodian of the grace of which I have been speaking in nonecclesiastical terms. At the same time it is a community of labor of sorts. The work addict is aided in laying hold of this gift if the gospel he receives is not all demand, rules, and law. He is made whole by a balance of these with promise, support, rest, and renewal. I wonder if this may not be one reason that music has been such a vital part of the heritage of the great faiths of our times. Music assures, supports, and relaxes a person at the same time it challenges, stirs, and commands him.

Habit-Reconditioning: The New Work of the Workaholic

With all the help that he can get—at home, on the job, and at church—the workaholic's new assignment is a sublimation of his need to work. He works at *not* working. He reconditions his habits day by day. The many suggestions I have made call for a campaign of habit-change, itself a kind of effort, or work. Behavior *can* be changed. *You can decide to change and do so*. This takes the same kind of commitment to doing a job that you have known before. Indeed, it is an application of the same energy in the opposite direction. Likewise, because you are in a position to spot work addiction in others, you will find plenty of company in your efforts. So go not alone, and may God also go with you.

Bibliography

Bell, Daniel. *Work and Its Discontents.* Boston: Beacon Press, 1958.

Clinebell, Howard J. and Clinebell, Charlotte H. *The Intimate Marriage.* New York: Harper & Row, 1970.

Cuber, John F. and Harroff, Peggy B. *The Significant Americans.* New York: Appleton-Century, 1965.

De Grazia, Sebastian. *Of Time, Work and Leisure.* New York: Twentieth Century Fund, 1962.

Deutsch, Helene. *The Psychology of Women.* 2 Vols. New York: Grune and Stratton, 1945.

Frankl, Viktor. *The Search for Meaning.* Boston: Beacon Press, 1963.

Howe, Reuel. *The Creative Years.* Greenwich, Conn.: Seabury Press, 1959.

Keen, Sam. *The Dance of Life.* New York: Harper & Row, 1970.

Keniston, Kenneth. *The Uncommitted.* New York: Harcourt, Brace & World, 1965.

Lindbergh, Anne Morrow. *Gift from the Sea.* New York: Pantheon, 1955.

Mead, Margaret. *Culture and Commitment: A Study of the Generation Gap.* Garden City, N.Y.: Doubleday, 1970.

Neale, Robert. *In Praise of Play.* New York: Harper & Row, 1970.

Sherrill, Lewis. *The Struggle of the Soul*. New York: Macmillan, 1951.

Smigel, Edward O. *Work and Leisure*. New Haven Conn.: College and University Press, 1963.

Steere, Douglas. *Work and Contemplation*. New York: Harper & Bros., 1957.